BREAD MACHINE COOKBOOK FOR BEGINNERS

Turn your kitchen into a bakery. How to get your healthy, fragrant and delicious bread without effort and in a cheaper way

Zea Heptinstall

Copyright © 2023 by Zea Heptinstall

All rights reserved.

No portion of this book may be reproduced in any form without written permission from the publisher or author, except as permitted by U.S. copyright law.

Table of Contents

INTRODUCTION **8**
    THE ALLURING SCENT OF FRESHLY MADE BREAD 8
    THE HEALTHIER CHOICE 8
    THE ECONOMICAL ADVANTAGE 9

DEMYSTIFYING THE BREAD MACHINE **10**
    EMBRACING THE BREAD MACHINE REVOLUTION 10
    UNDERSTANDING BREAD MACHINE TYPES 10
    UNBOXING AND SETTING UP YOUR MACHINE 11

INGREDIENTS **12**
    A GUIDE TO SELECTING AND STORING KEY INGREDIENTS 12
        Flour *12*
        Water *12*
        Yeast *12*
        Salt *12*
        Sweeteners *12*
        Fats *13*
    FLOUR VARIETIES AND THEIR IMPACT ON BREAD TEXTURE 13
    THE YEAST FACTOR: DRY, FRESH, AND ALTERNATIVES 14
        Dry Yeast *14*
        Fresh Yeast *14*
        Alternatives *14*
    THE ART OF MEASURING: PRECISION MATTERS 14

THE ORGANIC AND BUDGET-FRIENDLY APPROACH **15**
    BENEFITS OF ORGANIC INGREDIENTS IN BREAD-MAKING 15
    STRATEGIES TO BAKE ORGANIC WITHOUT BREAKING THE BANK 15
    HOMEMADE VERSUS STORE-BOUGHT: A COST AND HEALTH ANALYSIS 16

BREAD BAKING BASICS **18**
    UNDERSTANDING BREAD MACHINE CYCLES AND SETTINGS 18
    HOW TO READ THE RECIPES 19
    FIRST-TIME BAKING: YOUR STARTER RECIPE 20
    BASIC WHITE BREAD 20

CLASSIC AND SAVORY BREAD **21**
    WHOLE WHEAT BREAD 21
    MULTIGRAIN BREAD 22
    OATMEAL BREAD 23
    RYE BREAD 24
    SOURDOUGH BREAD 24
    GREEK YOGURT BREAD 25
    ITALIAN BREAD 26
    FRENCH BAGUETTE 27
    HERB AND GARLIC BREAD 28
    PUMPERNICKEL BREAD 29
    SUN-DRIED TOMATO BREAD 30
    OLIVE BREAD 31
    POTATO BREAD 32
    7-GRAIN BREAD 32
    FLAXSEED BREAD 33
    ROSEMARY FOCACCIA 34
    JALAPEÑO CHEDDAR BREAD 35

Irish Soda Bread	36
Buttermilk Bread	37
Pumpkin Bread	38
Parmesan Cheese Bread	39
Parmesan Rosemary Bread	40
Vegetable Infused Multigrain Bread	41
Poppy Seed Bread	42
Pesto Bread	43
Onion and Dill Bread	43
Spinach and Feta Bread	44
Caprese Bread	44
Bacon Cheddar Bread	45
Olive Rosemary Bread	45
Asiago and Sun-Dried Tomato Bread	46

SWEET SENSATION 47

Cinnamon Swirl Bread	47
Cinnamon Raisin Bread	48
Lemon Zucchini Bread	49
Blueberry Lemon Bread	50
Sweet Potato Bread	51
Chocolate Chip Bread	51
Amish Friendship Bread	52
Blueberry Muffin Bread	53
Banana Nut Bread	53
Cranberry Walnut Bread	54
Almond Poppy Seed Bread	54
Cranberry Orange Bread	55
Nutella Swirl Bread	55
Apple Cinnamon Bread	56
Maple Pecan Bread	56
Fig and Walnut Bread	57
Cherry Almond Bread	57
Cherry Chocolate Bread	58
Coconut Pineapple Bread	59
Apricot Ginger Bread	60
Raspberry White Chocolate Bread	60
Orange Poppy Seed Bread	61
Pumpkin Chocolate Swirl Bread	62

INTERNATIONAL BREAD ADVENTURE 63

Naan Bread	63
Greek Pita Bread	64
Mexican Tortilla Bread	65
Swedish Limpa Bread	66
Italian Ciabatta	67
Japanese Hokkaido Milk Bread	68
Russian Borodinsky Bread	68
Cuban Bread	69
Irish Brown Bread	69
Indian Roti	70
Ethiopian Injera	71
Portuguese Cornbread	71
Norwegian Kringle Bread	72
Armenian Lavash Bread	73
Moroccan Khobz Bread	73
Turkish Pide Bread	74

- Brazilian Pao de Queijo 75
- Peruvian Pan de Chancay 76
- German Pretzel Bread 77
- Argentinian Empanada Bread 78
- Jewish Challah 79

DIET-SPECIFIC BREAD 80

- Gluten-free Bread 80
- Low-Carb Almond Bread 81
- Vegan Black Sesame and Matcha Swirl Bread 82
- Keto Seed Bread 83
- Paleo Coconut Bread 84
- Low-Fat Oat Bread 85
- High-Fiber Avocado and Oat Bran Bread 86
- Diabetic-Friendly Cinnamon Bread 87
- Low-Sodium Apple Cinnamon Bread 88
- Low-Calorie Vegetable Bread 89
- High-Protein Quinoa Bread 89
- Nut-Free Sunflower Bread 90
- Soy-Free Tofu Bread 90
- Rice Flour Shokupan Bread 91
- No-Sugar Added Fruit Bread 92
- Heart-Healthy Oat Bran Bread 92
- Lactose-Free Potato Bread 93
- Candida-Friendly Coconut Flour Bread 94
- Nut-Free Sweet Potato Bread 95
- FODMAP-Friendly Spelt Bread 95
- Sibo Diet Cassava Bread 96
- Mediterranean Diet Fig and Walnut Bread with Feta 97
- South Beach Diet Flaxseed Bread 98
- Atkins Diet Cauliflower Bread 98
- DASH Diet Multigrain Bread with Seeds and Nuts.. 99
- Weight Watchers Friendly Chia and Honey Bread 100
- High-Fiber Psyllium Bread.. 101
- Thyroid-Friendly Seaweed Bread 101
- Celiac-Friendly Teff Bread 102
- Anti-Inflammatory Turmeric Bread 102

DOUGH BEYOND BREAD.. 103

- Pizza Dough 103
- Dinner Rolls 104
- Bagel Dough.. 105
- Spinach and Feta Stuffed Bread Dough 106
- Focaccia Dough 107
- English Muffin Dough 108
- Croissant Dough 109
- Danish Pastry Dough 109
- Whole Wheat Pita Bread with Flaxseed and Herbs Dough 110
- Flatbread Dough 111
- Scone Dough 112
- Thai Coconut Bread Dough... 113
- Dumpling Dough 114
- Waffle Batter Dough 114

CHALLENGES, MISTAKES, AND REMEDIES... 115

- Common Beginner Mistakes and How to Avoid Them 115
- Tackling Bread Failures: From Dense Loaves to Uncooked Centers.. 116

CONNECTING WITH THE BREAD-MAKING COMMUNITY 118
- Websites, Blogs, and Forums: Your Go-To Online Resources 118
- Podcasts and Influencers to Inspire Your Baking Journey 118

CONCLUSION: EMBRACING THE BREAD-MAKING JOURNEY 120
- The Art and Science of Bread: A Beautiful Balance 120
- Encouraging Continuous Learning and Experimentation 120

APPENDIX 121
- Glossary of Bread-Making Terms 121
- Conversion Table 122

❈ I HAVE A FREE GIFT FOR YOU! ❈

👇 SCAN HERE TO DOWNLOAD IT 👇

- Use your freshly baked bread from your bread machine
- Elevate your bread experience with a collection of sandwich recipes
- Amaze your family or friends with the perfect taste

Introduction

There is something undeniably magical about the scent of freshly made bread wafting through your home. It is a scent that evokes warmth, comfort, and nostalgia, triggering memories of cozy family gatherings, Sunday mornings, and simpler times. For many, the idea of making bread from scratch might seem daunting, but with the advent of the bread machine, this delightful experience has become more accessible than ever. Here, we will explore the joys of homemade bread, with a particular focus on the tantalizing scent it produces, while also delving into the benefits of embracing the bread machine revolution. Not only is homemade bread a sensory delight, but it is also a healthier and more economical choice.

The Alluring Scent of Freshly Made Bread

The aroma of freshly baked bread is one of life's simple delight. It has a unique ability to stir emotions and conjure up fond memories. As you enter a home where bread is being made, the scent engulfs you, making it nearly impossible to resist. But what is it about this fragrance that is so captivating?

1. **Warmth and Comfort:** the scent of fresh bread baking in the oven is like a warm hug for your senses. It envelops you in a cocoon of comfort and makes your home feel inviting and cozy. In a world filled with hustle and bustle, the simple act of baking bread can bring a sense of calm and tranquility.
2. **Nostalgia:** for many of us, the scent of bread baking in the oven instantly transports us to our childhood or to our grandparents' kitchen. It's a reminder of simpler times when life moved at a slower pace, and meals were made with love and care. The scent of bread connects us to our roots and traditions.
3. **Anticipation:** the scent of bread baking is incredibly tantalizing. It teases your senses, and as the aroma intensifies, you can't help but eagerly anticipate the first slice. The anticipation of that warm, freshly baked bread is a delightful experience in itself.
4. **Homemade Goodness:** unlike store-bought bread, the scent of homemade bread is distinct. It is a reminder that what you're about to relish is made with real, wholesome components. It carries the promise of homemade goodness and a taste that is unlike anything else.

The Healthier Choice

In addition to the sensory pleasure, homemade bread offers several health benefits, particularly when compared to commercial bread. Here is why you should consider making your own bread:

1. **Control over ingredients:** once you make your own bread, you have complete control over the components. You can choose high-quality flour, include seeds or grains for extra nutrition, and omit artificial additives and preservatives commonly found in commercial bread.
2. **Reduced sodium:** many store-bought bread varieties are loaded with sodium to enhance flavor and shelf life. Homemade bread allows you to regulate the salt content, making it a healthier choice for those watching their sodium intake.
3. **No hidden sugars:** commercial bread often contains hidden sugars that can be harmful to your health. Once you make your own bread, you can eliminate or reduce sugar, making it a better option for those looking to decrease their sugar intake.
4. **Whole grains:** homemade bread can simply incorporate whole grains, adding fiber and essential nutrients to your diet. Whole grains are known for their role in heart health and weight management.

5. **Freshness:** there is no substitute for the freshness of homemade bread. You can relish it at its peak, with all the nutrients and flavors intact.
6. **Dietary restrictions:** homemade bread is ideal for people with dietary restrictions or allergies. You can customize the recipe to suit your needs, whether it is gluten-free, vegan, or low-carb.

The Economical Advantage

Not only is homemade bread a healthier choice, but it is also an economical one. Here's how investing in a bread machine can save you money in the long run:

1. **Cost-Effective ingredients:** the basic components for bread - flour, water, yeast, and salt - are among the most affordable staples you can find. Making bread at home is cost-effective, especially when you consider the price of a high-quality loaf in a store.
2. **Customization:** a bread machine allows you to create a wide variety of bread types and flavors. By making your own bread, you can avoid the premium price tags attached to artisanal or specialty bread in the market.
3. **Reduced food waste:** you can make bread in small or big batches, ensuring that you have just the right amount for your needs. This reduces food waste and saves you from discarding half-eaten loaves.
4. **Energy efficiency:** modern bread machines are designed to be energy-efficient. Baking bread at home is often more energy-efficient than purchasing pre-made bread that has been shipped and stored.
5. **Convenience:** the convenience of a bread machine means you can have fresh bread whenever you want it, which can save you from buying expensive ready-made sandwiches or dining out.

Demystifying the Bread Machine

Bread machines have become a popular kitchen appliance, offering a convenient way to relish the pleasures of homemade bread. In this chapter, we will demystify the world of bread machines, helping you understand the different types available and guiding you through the unboxing and setup process.

Embracing the Bread Machine Revolution

The bread machine has revolutionized the way we make bread at home. It is a kitchen appliance that automates the bread-making process, making it accessible even to those with limited baking experience. Here are some reasons why you should consider embracing the bread machine revolution:

1. **Simplified process:** bread machines take the guesswork out of baking. You don't need to be an expert baker to produce delicious loaves. Most bread machines have user-friendly controls and preset programs for various types of bread.
2. **Time-Saving:** making bread from scratch traditionally can be a time-consuming task. With a bread machine, you can relish fresh bread with minimal effort. Simply include the components, select your desired settings, and let the machine do the work.
3. **Consistency:** bread machines are designed to produce consistent results every time. Your homemade bread will have the same great taste, texture, and aroma without the risk of human error.
4. **Versatility:** bread machines can do more than just bake bread. Many models have settings for making dough, pasta, and even jams. This versatility allows you to experiment with different recipes and extend your culinary knowledge.
5. **Cost-Effective:** while bread machines are an initial investment, they quickly pay for themselves through the savings you will relish by making your own bread. You will also avoid the temptation of purchasing pricier artisanal bread.
6. **Freshness:** bread machines ensure that your bread is as fresh as it can be. You can wake up to the scent of freshly made bread in the morning.
7. **Health control:** with a bread machine, you can monitor the components in your bread, ensuring it aligns with your dietary preferences and restrictions.
8. **Learning experience:** using a bread machine is a great way to learn the basics of bread making. As you become more comfortable with the process, you can experiment with different components and create unique recipes.

Understanding Bread Machine Types

Bread machines come in various types, each offering standard or customized functions. Understanding these distinctions can help you choose the one that best suits your needs.

- **Basic Bread Machines:** these models are designed for straightforward bread making. They typically offer settings for different types of bread (white, whole wheat, etc.) and various loaf sizes. Basic machines are great for beginners and those who prefer simpleness.
- **Convection Bread Machines:** convection bread machines incorporate a built-in fan that circulates hot air to ensure a quicker baking. This feature is particularly useful if you want a consistent crust on your bread.

- **Programmable Bread Machines:** these models provide more customization options, allowing you to create your own recipes and experiment with different ingredients. They often come with delay timers, set the alarm, so you can have fresh bread ready when you wake up or come home from work.
- **Gluten-free Bread Machines:** if you have dietary restrictions, consider a machine designed specifically for gluten-free recipes. These machines avoid cross-contamination and ensure gluten-free bread is safe for consumption.

Unboxing and Setting Up Your Machine

Once you have selected the bread machine that aligns with your preferences, it's time to unbox and set it up. Here is a step-by-step guide to help you get started:

1. **Unboxing:** carefully unbox your bread machine, making sure to take out all packaging materials. Check the user manual, as it often contains crucial information regarding initial setup and usage.
2. **Location:** choose a suitable location for your bread machine. It should be placed on a clean, level surface with good ventilation, away from direct sunlight, and other heat sources.
3. **Assembling:** insert the bread pan into the machine. Ensure it locks securely in place.
4. **Ingredients:** familiarize yourself with the components and recipes. It is essential to follow recipes carefully, especially when you're new to bread making.
5. **Control Panel:** study the control panel of your bread machine. Understand the different buttons, settings, and displays. The most common settings include the type of bread (e.g., white, whole wheat, sweet), crust color, and loaf size.

    Loaf size is determined by weight, as following:

    1 lb = small loaf size   1.5 lb = medium loaf size   2 lb = large loaf size

    Here a tip to finding out your machine's size, if this is not indicated on the user manual.

    Fill in the volume of the baking pan with some water: if it holds less than 12 cups, the bread machine will bake a 1 lb loaf, if it holds between 12 and 14 cups is a 1.5 lb loaf otherwise is a 2 lb loaf.

6. **Adding ingredients:** follow your chosen recipe, adding components in the order specified (usually liquids first, then dry components, and yeast last). Some machines have a separate compartment for adding nuts, seeds, or fruits.
7. **Start the Machine:** close the lid, select your desired settings, and start the machine. The bread machine will mix, knead, rise, and bake the bread automatically according to your chosen settings.
8. **Be Patient:** most bread machines take a couple of hours to complete the baking cycle. During this time, you will be treated to the delightful aroma of bread baking.

Ingredients

Baking exceptional bread is an art, and the key to mastering this art lies in understanding the components that form the foundation of your loaves. In this chapter, we will delve into the critical aspects of selecting and storing components, explore the various types of flour and their impact on bread texture, demystify the yeast factor (dry, fresh, and alternatives), and emphasize the importance of precision in measurement.

A Guide to Selecting and Storing Key Ingredients

The quality of your bread largely depends on the components you use, and the freshness and storage of these components can make a significant difference.

Flour
- **Selecting:** choose high-quality, unbleached all-purpose or bread flour. Look for brands that have a consistent reputation for producing reliable results. For specific bread types, like whole wheat or rye, opt for the corresponding flours.
- **Storing:** store flour in an airtight container in a cool, dry place. Flour can become rancid if exposed to moisture or heat. For longer storage, consider keeping flour in the freezer. To freeze flour, transfer it from its original packaging to an airtight plastic or glass container. Take out extra air to prevent freezer burn, either by using a vacuum sealer or placing plastic wrap directly on the flour's surface prior to sealing the container. Label the container with the freezing date and store it in the freezer for up to two years. For the best quality, use the flour within the first year, ensuring your baked goods maintain their optimal taste and texture.

Water
- **Selecting:** use filtered or tap water that is free of strong odors or impurities.
- **Storing:** there is no need to store water. Simply use it at the temp. specified in your recipe.

Yeast
- **Selecting:** for dry yeast, ensure it is fresh, and check the expiration date on the package. If you are using fresh yeast, purchase it from a reliable source.
- **Storing:** keep dry yeast in the fridge or freezer to prolong its shelf life. Fresh yeast should be refrigerated and used promptly. Both types should be sealed in an airtight container to avoid moisture and odors from affecting them.

Salt
- **Selecting:** regular table salt or kosher salt is suitable for bread making. Avoid using specialty salts with distinct flavors.
- **Storing:** salt is non-perishable and can be stored in any cool, dry put inside a firmly sealed container.

Sweeteners
- **Selecting:** honey, sugar, or malt extract are commonly used sweeteners in bread recipes. Choose one that aligns with your desired flavor profile.
- **Storing:** sweeteners have a long shelf life. Store them in a cool, dry place, away from moisture and insects.

Fats
- **Selecting:** common fats used in bread making include butter, olive oil, and vegetable oil. Choose the one that complements your recipe. Butter adds richness, while oils can lend moisture to the crumb.
- **Storing:** keep fats in their original containers or airtight containers in the fridge or a cool pantry, depending on the fat used.

Flour Varieties and Their Impact on Bread Texture

Flour is the primary ingredient in bread, and the type of flour you select greatly influences the texture and flavor of your loaves. Here is a brief overview of different flour varieties and their characteristics:

1. **All-Purpose Flour:** all-purpose flour is versatile and suitable for a wide range of bread recipes. It strikes a balance between protein content and texture, making it a reliable choice for many home bakers.
2. **Bread Flour:** bread flour has a higher protein content, typically around 11-14%. This extra protein results in a higher gluten formation, which leads to a chewier and more structured crumb. It is ideal for classic bread recipes and artisanal loaves.
3. **Whole Wheat Flour:** whole wheat flour is milled from the entire wheat kernel, including the bran and germ. It has a nutty flavor and a coarser texture. Using whole wheat flour results in denser, heartier bread with a rich, earthy flavor.
4. **Rye Flour:** rye flour is known for its distinct flavor, making it a favorite for rye bread and pumpernickel. It can be mixed with other flours to create a unique, tangy loaf.
5. **Spelt Flour:** spelt flour, an ancient grain, has a nutty, mildly sweet flavor. It is often used for specialty bread and is known for its excellent nutritional profile.
6. **Almond Flour:** almond flour, made from ground almonds, is gluten-free and imparts a rich, nutty flavor to bread. It is a favorite choice for those seeking gluten-free and low-carb alternatives.
7. **Coconut Flour:** coconut flour, derived from dried coconut meat, is highly absorbent and requires additional moisture in recipes. It has a sweet, tropical flavor and is commonly used in gluten-free and paleo baking for a unique taste experience.
8. **Sorghum Flour:** sorghum flour, produced from the sorghum grain, is a gluten-free alternative with a mild, mildly sweet flavor. It can be used in gluten-free baking to create soft, moist bread.
9. **Rice Flour:** rice flour, available in white and brown varieties, is gluten-free and imparts a neutral flavor to bread. It is an excellent choice for those with gluten sensitivities, contributing to a light, airy crumb.
10. **Teff Flour:** teff is a tiny, nutrient-packed grain that imparts a mildly nutty flavor and a dense, earthy texture to bread. It is a staple in Ethiopian cuisine and can include a unique twist to your bread recipes.

The choice of flour should align with your bread-making goals. Experimenting with different flours can lead to exciting results and diverse textures.

The Yeast Factor: Dry, Fresh, and Alternatives

Yeast is the magical microorganism responsible for bread's rise. Understanding the types of yeast and their characteristics is crucial for successful bread making.

Dry Yeast

- *Characteristics:* dry yeast is available in two primary forms, active dry yeast and instant yeast. Active dry yeast requires proofing in warm water prior to use, while instant yeast can be mixed directly with dry components. Both types provide consistent and reliable results.
- *Advantages:* long shelf life, ease of use, and reliability.

Fresh Yeast

- *Characteristics:* fresh yeast, also known as cake yeast or compressed yeast, is perishable and must be used promptly. It requires dissolution in warm water and is favored by some professional bakers for its unique fermentation properties.
- *Advantages:* offers a distinct flavor and texture to bread.

Alternatives

- *Sourdough Starter:* sourdough starter is a natural yeast culture that imparts a unique flavor and texture to bread. It requires regular feeding and maintenance, but the results are deeply satisfying.
- *Wild Yeast:* you can capture wild yeast from your environment to create a natural leaven for your bread. This process involves capturing airborne wild yeast and nurturing it to use in your recipes.

The choice of yeast depends on your preference and the specific recipe. Both dry yeast and fresh yeast are readily available and produce excellent results, making them the go-to choices for most home bakers.

The Art of Measuring: Precision Matters

Bread making is a science, and precision in measuring components is crucial. Here are some tips for accurate measurements:

1. **Use a digital scale:** weighing components using a digital kitchen scale provides the highest level of precision. It eliminates variations caused by differences in volume due to factors like humidity and packing.
2. **Use the Spoon-and-Level method:** once measuring flour, use a spoon to fill the measuring cup, then level it off with a flat edge. Avoid scooping directly from the flour bag, which can lead to packed and inaccurate measurements.
3. **Be consistent:** use the same measuring tools and techniques each time you bake. Consistency in measuring helps maintain the reliability of your recipes.
4. **Measure liquids at eye level:** once measuring liquids, ensure the meniscus (the curved surface of the liquid) is at the measurement line on the measuring cup. View it at eye level for accuracy.
5. **Sift flour if necessary:** some recipes call for sifted flour. Sifting helps prevent lumps and ensures even distribution. Sift the flour prior to measuring for precise amounts.
6. **Read the recipe carefully:** carefully follow the recipe's instructions and measurements. Deviating from the specified measurements can lead to unexpected results.

The Organic and Budget-Friendly Approach

Once it comes to bread making, the choice of components can significantly impact the final product's flavor, texture, and overall quality. Organic components have gained approval due to their perceived health benefits and reduced environmental impact. In this chapter, we will explore the benefits of using organic components in bread-making, discuss strategies to bake organic without breaking the bank, and conduct a cost and health analysis comparing homemade organic bread to store-bought alternatives.

Benefits of Organic Ingredients in Bread-Making
Health Benefits

- **Reduced Chemical Residues:** organic components are grown without the use of pesticides and genetically modified organisms (GMOs). This means lower exposure to potentially harmful chemical residues.
- **Nutrient-Rich:** organic grains and flours often have higher nutrient levels, which can result in a more nutritious loaf of bread. You will find increased levels of vitamins, minerals, and antioxidants in organic components.
- **No Artificial Additives:** organic bread components typically exclude artificial additives, preservatives, and artificial colors, which can have adverse health effects.

Environmental Benefits

- **Sustainable Agriculture:** organic farming practices are generally more sustainable and environmentally friendly. They promote soil health and reduce pollution.
- **Biodiversity:** organic farming encourages biodiversity and reduces the negative impact of monoculture on ecosystems.
- **No GMOs:** organic components are non-GMO, reducing the environmental and ethical concerns associated with genetically modified organisms.

Enhanced Flavor

- Many bread enthusiasts find that organic components offer a richer and more distinct flavor. The absence of artificial additives and the emphasis on natural cultivation can result in bread with a more authentic and delightful taste.

Strategies to Bake Organic Without Breaking the Bank
While organic components offer numerous benefits, they can be more expensive than conventional ones. Here are strategies to help you relish organic bread without straining your budget:

1. **Prioritize Key Ingredients:** focus on using organic components for key components of your bread, such as flour, while using conventional options for less significant components, like salt.
2. **Buy in Bulk:** purchasing organic components in bulk can significantly reduce the cost per unit. Many stores and online retailers offer discounts for buying larger quantities.
3. **Join a Co-op or Buying Club:** cooperative stores and buying clubs often provide access to organic components at lower prices. By pooling resources with others, you can relish cost savings.

4. **Shop Sales and Discounts:** keep an eye on sales, discounts, and coupons for organic components. Buying items on sale can save you a substantial amount over time.
5. **Consider Generic Brands:** generic or store brands of organic components are typically more affordable than well-known organic brands. Check the ingredient labels to ensure they meet your standards.
6. **Grow Your Own:** consider growing your own organic herbs or grains. Even a small home garden can provide you with some of the components you need.
7. **Buy Online:** online retailers often offer competitive prices for organic components, and you can take advantage of subscription services to save even more.

Homemade Versus Store-Bought: A Cost and Health Analysis

Let's compare homemade organic bread with store-bought options in terms of cost and health.

Cost Comparison

- **Homemade:** initially, investing in organic components for homemade bread may seem costlier. However, when you factor in the number of loaves you can produce from the components purchased in bulk, homemade bread becomes more cost-effective over time.
- **Store-Bought:** store-bought organic bread tends to be more expensive, as it includes production, packaging, and distribution costs. Buying it regularly can lead to higher overall expenses.

Health Comparison

- **Homemade:** making bread at home gives you control over the components and allows you to ensure they are fresh and of high quality. You can choose the finest organic components, create your recipes, and avoid additives, resulting in a healthier and more nutritious product.
- **Store-Bought:** store-bought organic bread may contain additives, preservatives, and stabilizers to prolong shelf life, which can diminish its overall health benefits. Additionally, you have less control over ingredient quality.

Customization

- **Homemade:** once you make bread at home, you can adapt recipes to suit your dietary preferences, creating variations like whole wheat, multigrain, or gluten-free loaves.
- **Store-Bought:** store-bought options have limited customization. You must choose from available varieties and may not find the perfect match for your dietary needs.

Freshness

- **Homemade:** homemade bread is fresher and can be enjoyed at its peak. The enticing aroma, warm crust, and soft crumb of a recently baked loaf are unmatched.
- **Store-Bought:** store-bought bread has a longer shelf life and may not offer the same level of freshness. While some options are baked locally and delivered fresh, others may spend days on store shelves.

Sustainability

- **Homemade:** making your bread at home can reduce packaging waste and lower your carbon footprint. You have control over sourcing sustainable and local components.

- **Store-Bought:** store-bought bread involves packaging and distribution, which is less environmentally friendly.

Bread Baking Basics

Bread baking is both an art and a science, and understanding the fundamentals is crucial to achieving that perfect loaf. In this chapter, we will explore the basics of bread baking, including a breakdown of bread machine cycles, settings and a beginner's starter recipe to get you on your way to bread-making mastery.

Understanding Bread Machine Cycles and Settings

Modern bread machines are designed to simplify the bread-making process, allowing even novices to produce consistently delicious loaves. To fully harness the power of your bread machine, it is essential to understand the various cycles it offers:

1. **Knead Cycle:** during this cycle, the bread machine mixes and kneads the components. It is essential for developing gluten and ensuring the dough's proper consistency. The duration of this cycle varies by machine, typically ranging from 10 to 20 minutes.

2. **Rise Cycle:** after kneading, the dough needs time to rise and double in size. This cycle can last anywhere from 30 minutes to 2 hours, depending on the bread machine. It is a crucial phase for flavor development and a light, airy texture.

3. **Punch-Down Cycle:** some bread machines include a punch-down cycle. During this phase, the machine will briefly knead the dough again to expel extra carbon dioxide and redistribute the yeast.

4. **Bake Cycle:** the bake cycle is where the magic happens. It is the longest part of the process and can last from 45 minutes to a couple of hours, depending on the type of bread and the crust color chosen. The bread machine heats up and maintains the proper temp. to bake the loaf to perfection.

5. **Keep Warm Cycle:** after baking, the bread machine often switches to a keep-warm cycle. This ensures your bread remains warm and fresh till you are ready to relish it.

Understanding and utilizing these cycles according to your recipe is essential for achieving the desired bread texture and flavor.

Having the right knowledge of the various settings on your machine is crucial. Each setting is designed to optimize the baking process for different types of bread and dough. Below is a concise table that explains the common settings you'll find on most bread machines, helping you to choose the right one for your recipe:

Setting	Description
Basic/Normal	This is the standard setting for most simple bread recipes, especially for white and mixed breads. It typically involves a medium baking time and crust color.
Whole Wheat	Specifically tailored for whole grain and wheat breads, this setting adjusts kneading and rising times to account for heavier dough consistency.
French	Ideal for recipes that require a longer kneading and rising period, resulting in a crispier crust. Perfect for French bread and other European varieties.
Sweet	Used for breads with higher sugar, fat, or protein content (like fruit or nut breads). It modifies the baking process to prevent burning or over-browning.
Gluten-free	A specialized setting for gluten-free bread recipes, accommodating the unique texture and ingredients often used in these breads.
Quick Bread	For recipes that do not use yeast and do not require rising time. Typically involves a shorter baking cycle.
Dough	A setting that prepares and kneads the dough but stops before baking. Ideal for dough intended for pizza, rolls, or to be baked in a conventional oven.
Bake Only	This setting skips the kneading and rising phases and only bakes. Useful for dough prepared outside the bread machine or for final baking after shaping.

How to Read the Recipes
Degree of Difficulty:

- ★☆☆☆☆ (1 star): Trivial
- ★★☆☆☆ (2 stars): Easy
- ★★★☆☆ (3 stars): Moderate
- ★★★★☆ (4 stars): Challenging
- ★★★★★ (5 stars): Expert

Because of the cooking process is mainly managed by the bread machine itself, you will find recipes with 2 or 3 stars of difficulties, not more.

Average Expense:

The range of expense provided for each recipe is a general estimate of the cost associated with preparing the dish. It is calculated based on the average market prices of the components and is meant to give you a rough idea of how much you might spend when making the recipe. However, please keep in mind that the actual cost may vary depending on factors such as brand choices, location, and market fluctuations. This expense range should present as a helpful reference to budget-conscious cooks.

Preparation time (no Cooking time):

The preparation time provided for each recipe is a general estimate of amount of active work you, as the baker, need to put in before the machine takes over.

The cooking time, unlike many other books, is not showed because it is managed automatically by the machine itself. When you select a specific setting (like "Basic," "Whole Wheat," "French," etc.), the bread machine automatically adjusts the timing for each phase of the bread-making process. This includes the initial mixing and kneading of the dough, the rising time, and the final baking.

Each setting is programmed to optimize the process based on the type of bread or dough being made

The automation of these processes is a key feature of bread machines, making them convenient and user-friendly, especially for beginners or those who want to enjoy freshly baked bread without the hands-on effort required in traditional baking methods. However, it's always good to consult the specific manual for your bread machine model, as functionalities and settings can vary.

Servings:

It refers to the number of individual portions the completed loaf of bread is expected to yield.

The quantity ingredients of each recipe has been considered for a medium size loaf (1.5 lb).

Keep in mind that bread machines can have slightly different capacities, so it's always good to refer to your specific machine's manual for the best results.

In the recipes is often used the active dry yeast but you can use also instant yeast but paying attention to use it mixed directly with other dry ingredients and using about 25% less than the quantity indicated for active dry yeast.

Each unique recipe offers you the opportunity to explore new flavors and techniques every 10 days, enriching your baking experience over the next three-plus years.

First-Time Baking: Your Starter Recipe

If you are just beginning your bread-making journey, starting with a basic recipe can provide a solid foundation for your future baking endeavors. Here is a simple starter recipe for a classic white bread:

Basic White Bread

Degree of difficulty: ★★☆☆☆   **Average expense:** $2-$3

Preparation time: 10 minutes   **Servings:** 1.5 lb loaf (12 slices)

Ingredients:

- 1 cup warm water (at a temp. around 110 deg.F)
- 2 1/4 teaspoons active dry yeast
- 3 cups all-purpose flour (or bread flour)
- 2 tablespoons olive oil
- 1 1/2 teaspoons salt

Directions:

1. Include warm water to the bread machine's pan.
2. Spray yeast across the water and allow it to relax for around 5 minutes until it becomes frothy.
3. Include olive oil, flour, and salt to the pan.
4. Put pan in the bread machine, choose the basic/normal setting, and start the machine.
5. Once baking cycle is complete, take out the bread and allow it to relax prior to slicing.

Per serving: Calories: 120kcal; Fat: 2g; Carbs: 22g; Protein: 3g

Classic and Savory Bread

This section is the heart and soul of bread-making, where we explore the timeless classics that have graced dining tables for generations and the everyday breads that have become a staple in households around the world.

Whole Wheat Bread

Degree of difficulty: ★★☆☆   **Average expense:** $3-$4

Preparation time: 10 minutes   **Servings:** 1.5 lb loaf (12 slices)

Ingredients:

- 1 1/4 cups warm water (at a temp. around 110 deg.F)
- 2 1/4 teaspoons active dry yeast
- 2 cups whole wheat flour
- 1 cup all-purpose flour (or bread flour)
- 2 tablespoons honey
- 1 1/2 teaspoons salt
- 2 tablespoons olive oil

Directions:

1. Include warm water to the bread machine's pan.
2. Spray yeast across the water and allow it to relax for around 5 minutes until it becomes frothy.
3. Include both types of flour, honey, salt, and olive oil to the pan.
4. Put pan in the bread machine, choose the whole wheat setting, and start the machine.
5. Once baking cycle is complete, take out the bread and allow it to relax prior to slicing.

Per serving: Calories: 160kcal; Fat: 3g; Carbs: 31g; Protein: 5g

Multigrain Bread

Degree of difficulty: ★★☆☆☆ **Average expense:** $3-$4

Preparation time: 10 minutes **Servings:** 1.5 lb loaf (12 slices)

Ingredients:

- 1 cup water (at a temp. around 110 deg.F)
- 2 1/4 teaspoons active dry yeast
- 2 cups bread flour
- 1 cup whole wheat flour
- 1/2 cup multigrain cereal
- 2 tablespoons brown sugar
- 1 teaspoon salt
- 2 tablespoons oil

Directions:

1. Include warm water to the bread machine's pan.
2. Spray yeast across the water and allow it to relax for around 5 minutes until it becomes frothy.
3. Include both types of flour, honey, salt, and olive oil to the pan.
4. Put pan in the bread machine, choose the basic/normal setting, and start the machine.
5. Once baking cycle is complete, take out the bread and allow it to relax prior to slicing.

Per serving: Calories: 170kcal; Fat: 3g; Carbs: 26g; Protein: 5g

Oatmeal Bread

Degree of difficulty: ★★☆☆☆ **Average expense:** $3-$4

Preparation time: 10 minutes **Servings:** 1.5 lb loaf (12 slices)

Ingredients:

- 1 1/4 cups warm water (at a temp. around 110 deg.F)
- 2 1/4 teaspoons active dry yeast
- 2 cups bread flour
- 1/2 cup rolled oats
- 2 tablespoons honey
- 1 1/2 teaspoons salt
- 2 tablespoons olive oil

Directions:

1. Include warm water to the bread machine's pan.
2. Spray yeast across the water and allow it to relax for around 5 minutes until it becomes frothy.
3. Include bread flour, rolled oats, honey, salt, and olive oil to the pan.
4. Put pan in the bread machine, choose the basic/normal setting, and start the machine.
5. Once baking cycle is complete, take out the bread and allow it to relax prior to slicing.

Per serving: Calories: 140kcal; Fat: 3g; Carbs: 26g; Protein: 4g

Rye Bread

Degree of difficulty: ★★☆☆☆ **Average expense:** $3-$4

Preparation time: 10 minutes **Servings:** 1.5 lb loaf (12 slices)

Ingredients:

- 1 1/3 cups warm water (at a temp. around 110 deg.F)
- 2 1/4 teaspoons active dry yeast
- 2 cups rye flour
- 1 cup bread flour
- 2 tablespoons honey
- 1 1/2 teaspoons salt
- 2 tablespoons olive oil
- 1 tablespoons caraway seeds (elective)

Directions:

1. Include warm water to the bread machine's pan.
2. Spray yeast across the water and allow it to relax for around 5 minutes until it becomes frothy.
3. Include rye flour, bread flour, honey, salt, olive oil, and caraway seeds (if using) to the pan.
4. Put pan in the bread machine, choose the whole wheat setting, and start the machine.
5. Once baking cycle is complete, take out the bread and allow it to relax prior to slicing.

Per serving: Calories: 150kcal; Fat: 3g; Carbs: 28g; Protein: 4g

Sourdough Bread

Degree of difficulty: ★★★☆☆ **Average expense:** $2-$3

Preparation time: 15 minutes **Servings:** 1.5 lb loaf (12 slices)

Ingredients:

- 1/2 cup warm water (at a temp. around 110 deg.F)
- 1 cup sourdough starter (active)
- 1 1/2 cups bread flour
- 1/2 cup whole wheat flour
- 1 1/2 teaspoons salt
- 2 tablespoons olive oil

Directions:

1. Include the sourdough starter, flours, salt, and olive oil to the bread machine's pan.
2. Slowly include the warm water while the machine is mixing.
3. Put pan in the bread machine, choose the basic/normal setting, and start the machine.
4. Once baking cycle is complete, take out the sourdough bread and allow it to relax prior to slicing.

Per serving: Calories: 120kcal; Fat: 2.5g; Carbs: 22g; Protein: 4g

Greek Yogurt Bread

Degree of difficulty: ★★☆☆☆ **Average expense:** $3-$4

Preparation time: 10 minutes **Servings:** 1.5 lb loaf (12 slices)

Ingredients:

- 1 cups warm water (at a temp. around 110 deg.F)
- 2 1/4 teaspoons active dry yeast
- 2 cups bread flour
- 1/2 cup whole wheat flour
- 1/2 cup Greek yogurt (plain and full-fat)
- 2 tablespoons honey
- 1 1/2 teaspoons salt
- 1 tablespoon olive oil

Directions:

5. Add the bread flour, whole wheat flour, active dry yeast, and salt to the bread machine's pan.
6. In a separate bowl, mix the warm water, Greek yogurt, honey, and olive oil. Once combined, add this mixture to the bread machine's pan.
7. Set the bread machine to the basic/normal setting and start the machine.
8. Once the baking cycle is complete, remove the Greek Yogurt Bread and allow it to cool before slicing.

Per serving: Calories: 140kcal; Fat: 2g; Carbs: 26g; Protein: 5g

Italian Bread

Degree of difficulty: ★★★☆☆

Average expense: $3-$4

Preparation time: 20 minutes

Servings: 1.5 lb loaf (12 slices)

Ingredients:

- 1 1/4 cups milk
- 2 1/4 teaspoons active dry yeast
- 3 1/2 cups bread flour
- 1 teaspoon salt
- 2 tablespoons olive oil

Directions:

1. Add milk to the bread machine's pan.
2. Bring bread flour, salt, olive oil and yeast to the pan.
3. Put pan in the bread machine, select the dough setting, and start the machine.
4. Once the cycle is complete, take out the dough and pour it onto a lightly floured surface.
5. Shape the loaf as a torpedo placing it in a baking sheet.
6. Let the torpedo rise for 1.5 hours.
7. After 1.5 hours, make with a knife some not deep diagonal slices on the top.
8. Place the loaf in the oven at 460 deg.F for 25 minutes, or until it turns golden brown.

Per serving: Calories: 130kcal; Fat: 2.5g; Carbs: 24g; Protein: 3g

French Baguette

Degree of difficulty: ★★★☆☆ **Average expense:** $2-$3

Preparation time: 20 minutes **Servings:** 1.5 lb loaf (12 slices)

Ingredients:

- 1 cup warm water (at a temp. around 110 deg.F)
- 2 1/4 teaspoons active dry yeast
- 2 1/2 cups bread flour
- 1 1/2 teaspoons salt

Directions:

1. Include warm water to the bread machine's pan.
2. Spray yeast across the water and allow it to relax for around 5 minutes until it becomes frothy.
3. Include bread flour and salt to the pan.
4. Put pan in the bread machine, choose the dough setting and start the machine.
5. Once the bread machine cycle is finished, take out the dough from the pan then place it on a mildly floured surface, like a clean countertop.
6. Gently punch down the dough to take out any extra air. Then, shape the dough into a long, thin cylinder, similar to a baguette shape. You can do this by wrapping the sides of the dough toward the center and rolling it up from one end to the other. Use your hands to stretch and shape the dough as needed.
7. Put the shaped baguette on a baking sheet or a baguette pan, seam side down. You can also use a baguette proofing cloth or a couche to support the dough's shape and prevent sticking.
8. Cover the baguette with a clean kitchen towel then let it rest and rise for around 30 minutes to 1 hour. During this time, the baguette will increase in size.
9. Warm up your oven to 450 deg.F during the last 20-30 minutes of the dough's resting period. If you have a baking stone or a pizza stone, put it inside the oven while preheating.
10. Optionally, you can make diagonal slashes (score) on the baguette's surface with a sharp knife or a razor blade just prior to baking. This helps the baguette expand properly during baking.
11. Put the baguette in the warmed up oven then bake for around 20-25 minutes, or till it turns golden brown and sounds hollow when you tap the bottom.
12. Take out the baguette from the oven then allow it to relax on a wire stand.

Per serving: Calories: 110kcal; Fat: 0.5g; Carbs: 22g; Protein: 4g

Herb and Garlic Bread

Degree of difficulty: ★★☆☆☆

Average expense: $3-$4

Preparation time: 15 minutes

Servings: 1.5 lb loaf (12 slices)

Ingredients:

- 1 cup warm water (at a temp. around 110 deg.F)
- 2 1/4 teaspoons active dry yeast
- 3 cups bread flour
- 2 tablespoons olive oil
- 2 tablespoons fresh herbs (e.g., rosemary, thyme, or oregano), finely severed
- 2 pieces garlic, crushed
- 1 1/2 teaspoons salt

Directions:

1. Include warm water to the bread machine's pan.
2. Spray yeast across the water for around 5 minutes until it becomes frothy.
3. Include bread flour, olive oil, fresh herbs, garlic, and salt to the pan.
4. Put pan in the bread machine, choose the basic/normal setting and start the machine.
5. Once baking cycle is complete, take out the herb and garlic bread and allow it to relax prior to slicing.

Per serving: Calories: 130kcal; Fat: 3g; Carbs: 24g; Protein: 4g

Pumpernickel Bread

Degree of difficulty: ★★☆☆☆
Average expense: $4-$5
Preparation time: 10 minutes
Servings: 1.5 lb loaf (12 slices)

Ingredients:

- 1 1/3 cups warm water (at a temp. around 110 deg.F)
- 2 1/4 teaspoons active dry yeast
- 1 1/2 cups rye flour
- 1 1/2 cups bread flour
- 2 tablespoons molasses
- 1 1/2 teaspoons salt
- 1/2 teaspoon caraway seeds (elective)

Directions:

1. Include warm water to the bread machine's pan.
2. Spray yeast across the water for around 5 minutes until it becomes frothy.
3. Include rye flour, bread flour, molasses, salt, and caraway seeds (if using) to the pan.
4. Put pan in the bread machine, choose the whole wheat setting, and start the machine.
5. Once baking cycle is complete, take out the pumpernickel bread and allow it to relax prior to slicing.

Per serving: Calories: 140kcal; Fat: 1g; Carbs: 30g; Protein: 4g

Sun-Dried Tomato Bread

Degree of difficulty: ★★☆☆☆ **Average expense:** $3-$4

Preparation time: 15 minutes **Servings:** 1.5 lb loaf (12 slices)

Ingredients:

- 1 1/4 cups warm water (at a temp. around 110 deg.F)
- 2 1/4 teaspoons active dry yeast
- 3 cups bread flour
- 1/2 cup sun-dried tomatoes, rehydrated and severed
- 2 tablespoons olive oil
- 1 1/2 teaspoons salt
- 1 teaspoon dried basil

Directions:

1. Include warm water to the bread machine's pan.
2. Spray yeast across the water for around 5 minutes until it becomes frothy.
3. Include bread flour, sun-dried tomatoes, olive oil, salt, and dried basil to the pan.
4. Put pan in the bread machine, choose the basic/normal setting and start the machine.
5. Once baking cycle is complete, take out the sun-dried tomato bread and allow it to relax prior to slicing.

Per serving: Calories: 140kcal; Fat: 2.5g; Carbs: 26g; Protein: 4g

Olive Bread

Degree of difficulty: ★★☆☆☆ **Average expense:** $3-$4

Preparation time: 15 minutes **Servings:** 1.5 lb loaf (12 slices)

Ingredients:

- 1 cup warm water (at a temp. around 110 deg.F)
- 2 1/4 teaspoons active dry yeast
- 3 cups bread flour
- 1/2 cup pitted black/green olives, carved
- 2 tablespoons olive oil
- 1 1/2 teaspoons salt
- 1 teaspoon dried rosemary

Directions:

1. Include warm water to the bread machine's pan.
2. Spray yeast across the water for around 5 minutes until it becomes frothy.
3. Include bread flour, olives, olive oil, salt, and dried rosemary to the pan.
4. Put pan in the bread machine, choose the basic/normal setting and start the machine.
5. Once baking cycle is complete, take out the olive bread and allow it to relax prior to slicing.

Per serving: Calories: 150kcal; Fat: 3g; Carbs: 25g; Protein: 4g

Potato Bread

Degree of difficulty: ★★☆☆☆ **Average expense:** $3-$4
Preparation time: 15 minutes **Servings:** 1.5 lb loaf (12 slices)
Ingredients:

- 1 cup warm water (at a temp. around 110 deg.F)
- 2 1/4 teaspoons active dry yeast
- 2 cups bread flour
- 1 cup mashed potatoes (cooled)
- 2 tablespoons olive oil
- 1 1/2 teaspoons salt
- 1 tablespoon dried chives (elective)

Directions:

1. Include warm water to the bread machine's pan.
2. Spray yeast across the water for around 5 minutes until it becomes frothy.
3. Include bread flour, mashed potatoes, olive oil, salt, and dried chives (if using) to the pan.
4. Put pan in the bread machine, choose the basic/normal setting, and start the machine.
5. Once baking cycle is complete, take out the potato bread and allow it to relax prior to slicing.

Per serving: Calories: 130kcal; Fat: 3g; Carbs: 28g; Protein: 4g

7-Grain Bread

Degree of difficulty: ★★☆☆☆ **Average expense:** $3-$4
Preparation time: 10 minutes **Servings:** 1.5 lb loaf (12 slices)
Ingredients:

- 1 1/4 cups warm water (at a temp. around 110 deg.F)
- 2 1/4 teaspoons active dry yeast
- 2 cups 7-grain cereal mix
- 1 1/2 cups bread flour
- 2 tablespoons honey
- 1 1/2 teaspoons salt

Directions:

1. Include warm water to the bread machine's pan.
2. Spray yeast across the water for around 5 minutes until it becomes frothy.
3. Include the 7-grain cereal mix, bread flour, honey, and salt to the pan.
4. Put pan in the bread machine, choose the whole wheat setting, and start the machine.
5. Once baking cycle is complete, take out the 7-grain bread and allow it to relax prior to slicing.

Per serving: Calories: 180kcal; Fat: 1g; Carbs: 37g; Protein: 7g

Flaxseed Bread

Degree of difficulty: ★★☆☆☆   **Average expense:** $3-$4

Preparation time: 10 minutes   **Servings:** 1.5 lb loaf (12 slices)

Ingredients:

- 1 1/4 cups warm water (at a temp. around 110 deg.F)
- 2 1/4 teaspoons active dry yeast
- 3 cups bread flour
- 1/2 cup ground flaxseed
- 2 tablespoons honey
- 2 tablespoons olive oil
- 1 1/2 teaspoons salt

Directions:

1. Include warm water to the bread machine's pan.
2. Spray yeast across the water for around 5 minutes until it becomes frothy.
3. Include bread flour, ground flaxseed, honey, olive oil, and salt to the pan.
4. Put pan in the bread machine, choose the basic/normal setting, and start the machine.
5. Once baking cycle is complete, take out the flaxseed bread and allow it to relax prior to slicing.

Per serving: Calories: 160kcal; Fat: 5g; Carbs: 25g; Protein: 5g

Rosemary Focaccia

Degree of difficulty: ★★★☆☆   **Average expense:** $2-$3

Preparation time: 20 minutes   **Servings:** 1.5 lb loaf (12 slices)

Ingredients:

- 1 cup warm water (at a temp. around 110 deg.F)
- 2 1/4 teaspoons active dry yeast
- 2 1/2 cups bread flour
- 2 tablespoons olive oil
- 1 1/2 teaspoons salt
- 1 teaspoon dried rosemary
- 1/4 teaspoon garlic powder (elective)
- Coarse sea salt for sprinkling

Directions:

1. Include warm water to the bread machine's pan.
2. Spray yeast across the water for around 5 minutes until it becomes frothy.
3. Include bread flour, olive oil, salt, dried rosemary, and garlic powder (optional) to the pan.
4. Put pan in the bread machine, choose the dough cycle, and start the machine.
5. Once cycle is complete, take out the dough, and press it into a oiled baking sheet, creating a flat, rectangular shape.
6. Cover the dough and let it rise for around 30 minutes.
7. Warm up oven to 375 deg. F, spray the dough with coarse sea salt, then bake for 20-25 minutes or until it is golden brown.
8. Let the focaccia cool prior to slicing.

Per serving: Calories: 140kcal; Fat: 3g; Carbs: 24g; Protein: 4g

Jalapeño Cheddar Bread

Degree of difficulty: ★★☆☆☆ **Average expense:** $3-$4

Preparation time: 15 minutes **Servings:** 1.5 lb loaf (12 slices)

Ingredients:

- 1 cup warm water (at a temp. around 110 deg.F)
- 2 1/4 teaspoons active dry yeast
- 3 cups bread flour
- 1 1/2 cups shredded cheddar cheese
- 1-2 jalapeño peppers, sowed and finely severed
- 2 tablespoons olive oil
- 1 1/2 teaspoons salt

Directions:

1. Include warm water to the bread machine's pan.
2. Spray yeast across the water for around 5 minutes until it becomes frothy.
3. Include bread flour, shredded cheddar cheese, jalapeño peppers, olive oil, and salt to the pan.
4. Put pan in the bread machine, choose the basic/normal setting, and start the machine.
5. Once baking cycle is complete, take out the Jalapeño Cheddar Bread and allow it to relax prior to slicing.

Per serving: Calories: 200kcal; Fat: 9g; Carbs: 22g; Protein: 7g

Irish Soda Bread

Degree of difficulty: ★★☆☆☆ **Average expense:** $2-$3

Preparation time: 15 minutes **Servings:** 1.5 lb loaf (12 slices)

Ingredients:

- 1 1/2 cups buttermilk
- 1 egg
- 2 tablespoons honey
- 2 cups whole wheat flour
- 2 cups all-purpose flour (or bread flour)
- 1 teaspoon baking soda
- 1 teaspoon salt

Directions:

1. Inside your blending container, whisk collectively buttermilk, egg, and honey.
2. Inside distinct container, blend whole wheat flour, all-purpose flour, baking soda, and salt.
3. Put wet components to dry components and mix till a dough forms.
4. Shape dough into a round loaf then put it inside the bread machine's oiled pan.
5. Select the quick bread setting on your bread machine.
6. Once baking cycle is complete, take out the Irish Soda Bread and allow it to relax prior to slicing.

Per serving: Calories: 180kcal; Fat: 1g; Carbs: 37g; Protein: 6g

Buttermilk Bread

Degree of difficulty: ★★☆☆☆

Average expense: $3-$4

Preparation time: 10 minutes

Servings: 1.5 lb loaf (12 slices)

Ingredients:

- 1 1/4 cups warm water (at a temp. around 110 deg.F)
- 2 1/4 teaspoons active dry yeast
- 3 cups bread flour
- 1/2 cup buttermilk
- 2 tablespoons honey
- 1 1/2 teaspoons salt

Directions:

1. Include warm water to the bread machine's pan.
2. Spray yeast across the water around 5 minutes until it becomes frothy.
3. Include bread flour, buttermilk, honey, and salt to the pan.
4. Put pan in the bread machine, choose the basic/normal bread setting and start the machine.
5. Once baking cycle is complete, take out the Buttermilk Bread and allow it to relax prior to slicing.

Per serving: Calories: 150kcal; Fat: 1.5g; Carbs: 30g; Protein: 5g

Pumpkin Bread

Degree of difficulty: ★★☆☆☆

Average expense: $3-$4

Preparation time: 15 minutes

Servings: 1.5 lb loaf (12 slices)

Ingredients:

- 1 1/4 cups tinned pumpkin puree
- 2 tablespoons olive oil
- 1/4 cup honey
- 1/2 cup warm water (at a temp. around 110 deg.F)
- 2 1/4 teaspoons active dry yeast
- 2 1/2 cups bread flour
- 1/2 teaspoon cinnamon
- 1/2 teaspoon nutmeg (optional)
- 1/2 teaspoon salt

Directions:

1. Inside small container, blend warm water and yeast, and allow it to relax for around 5 minutes until it becomes frothy.
2. Inside distinct container, mix pumpkin puree, olive oil, honey, cinnamon, nutmeg (if using), and salt.
3. Include yeast solution to the pumpkin solution.
4. Include bread flour to the solution gradually.
5. Put pan in the bread machine, choose basic/normal bread setting, and start the machine.
6. Once baking cycle is complete, take out the Pumpkin Bread and allow it to relax prior to slicing.

Per serving: Calories: 140kcal; Fat: 2g; Carbs: 27g; Protein: 4g

Parmesan Cheese Bread

Degree of difficulty: ★★☆☆☆

Average expense: $3-$4

Preparation time: 15 minutes

Servings: 1.5 lb loaf (12 slices)

Ingredients:

- 1 1/4 cups warm water (at a temp. around 110 deg.F)
- 2 1/4 teaspoons active dry yeast
- 3 cups bread flour
- 1/2 cup grated Parmesan cheese
- 2 tablespoons olive oil
- 1 1/2 teaspoons salt
- 1/2 teaspoon garlic powder
- 1/2 teaspoon dried basil

Directions:

1. Include warm water to the bread machine's pan.
2. Spray yeast across the water for around 5 minutes until it becomes frothy.
3. Include bread flour, grated Parmesan cheese, olive oil, salt, garlic powder, and dried basil to the pan.
4. Put pan in the bread machine, choose the basic/normal bread setting and start the machine.
5. Once baking cycle is complete, take out the Parmesan Cheese Bread and allow it to relax prior to slicing.

Per serving: Calories: 180kcal; Fat: 4g; Carbs: 29g; Protein: 6g

Parmesan Rosemary Bread

Degree of difficulty: ★★☆☆☆

Average expense: $3-$4

Preparation time: 15 minutes

Servings: 1.5 lb loaf (12 slices)

Ingredients:

- 1 1/2 cups warm water (at a temp. around 110 deg.F)
- 2 teaspoons active dry yeast
- 3 cups bread flour
- 1 1/2 teaspoon salt
- 1 1/2 teaspoon sugar
- 1/2 cup grated Parmesan cheese
- 2 tablespoons fresh rosemary, severed
- 1 teaspoon garlic powder

Directions:

1. Include warm water to the bread machine's pan.
2. Spray yeast across the water for around 5 minutes until it becomes frothy.
3. Include bread flour, grated Parmesan cheese, sugar, salt, garlic powder, and fresh rosemary to the pan.
4. Put pan in the bread machine, choose the basic/normal bread setting and start the machine.
5. Once baking cycle is complete, take out the Parmesan Rosemary Bread and allow it to relax prior to slicing.

Per serving: Calories: 190kcal; Fat: 4g; Carbs: 29g; Protein: 6g

Vegetable Infused Multigrain Bread

Degree of difficulty: ★★☆☆☆ **Average expense:** $3-$4

Preparation time: 15 minutes **Servings:** 1.5 lb loaf (12 slices)

Ingredients:

- 1 1/4 cups water (at a temp. around 110 deg.F)
- 2 1/4 teaspoons active dry yeast
- 2 cups whole wheat flour
- 1 cup multigrain flour (or additional whole wheat flour)
- 2 tablespoons olive oil
- 1/4 cup organic carrot, finely grated
- 1/4 cup organic zucchini, finely grated (excess moisture squeezed out)
- 2 tablespoons tomato paste
- 2 tablespoons ground flaxseed
- 1 1/2 teaspoons salt

Directions:

1. Add the warm water, olive oil, grated carrot, zucchini, and tomato paste to the bread machine pan. Stir to combine.
2. Add the whole wheat flour and multigrain flour on top of the wet ingredients.
3. Sprinkle the ground flaxseed and salt over the flour.
4. Make a small indentation in the flour and add the yeast.
5. Select whole wheat bread setting on your bread machine and start the bread machine.
6. Once the baking cycle is complete, carefully remove the bread from the machine and let it cool before slicing.

Per serving: Calories: 160kcal; Fat: 3.5g; Carbs: 26g; Protein: 4g

Poppy Seed Bread

Degree of difficulty: ★★☆☆☆ **Average expense:** $2-$3

Preparation time: 15 minutes **Servings:** 1.5 lb loaf (12 slices)

Ingredients:

- 1 1/4 cups warm water (at a temp. around 110 deg.F)
- 2 1/4 teaspoons active dry yeast
- 3 cups bread flour
- 1/4 cup honey
- 1/4 cup poppy seeds
- 2 tablespoons olive oil
- 1 1/2 teaspoons salt
- 1/2 teaspoon lemon zest (optional)

Directions:

1. Include warm water to the bread machine's pan.
2. Spray yeast across the water for around 5 minutes until it becomes frothy.
3. Include bread flour, honey, poppy seeds, olive oil, salt, and lemon zest (if using) to the pan.
4. Put pan in the bread machine, choose the basic/normal bread setting, and start the machine.
5. Once baking cycle is complete, take out the Poppy Seed Bread and allow it to relax prior to slicing.

Per serving: Calories: 150kcal; Fat: 3.5g; Carbs: 27g; Protein: 4g

Pesto Bread

Degree of difficulty: ★★★☆☆ **Average expense:** $3-$4

Preparation time: 15 minutes **Servings:** 1.5 lb loaf (12 slices)

Ingredients:

- 1 cup warm water (at a temp. around 110 deg.F)
- 2 1/4 teaspoons active dry yeast
- 3 cups whole wheat flour
- 2 tablespoons olive oil
- 2 tablespoons pesto sauce

Directions:

1. Include warm water and yeast to the bread machine. Allow yeast to bloom for 5-10 minutes.
2. Include whole wheat flour, olive oil, pesto sauce to the machine.
3. Set the bread machine to the basic/normal setting and start the cycle.
4. Once baking cycle is complete, take out the Pesto Bread and allow it to relax prior to slicing.

Per serving: Calories: 150kcal; Fat: 3g; Carbs: 26g; Protein: 4g

Onion and Dill Bread

Degree of difficulty: ★★☆☆☆ **Average expense:** $3-$4

Preparation time: 15 minutes **Servings:** 1.5 lb loaf (12 slices)

Ingredients:

- 1 cup warm water (at a temp. around 110 deg.F)
- 2 1/4 teaspoons active dry yeast
- 3 cups whole wheat flour
- 2 tablespoons olive oil
- 1/4 cup finely severed onions
- 1 tablespoon dried dill

Directions:

1. Include warm water and yeast to the bread machine. Allow yeast to bloom for 5-10 minutes.
2. Include flour, olive oil, severed onions, and dried dill to the machine.
3. Set the bread machine to the basic/normal setting and start the cycle.
4. Once baking cycle is complete, take out the Onion and Dill Bread and allow it to relax prior to slicing.

Per serving: Calories: 140kcal; Fat: 3g; Carbs: 24g; Protein: 4.5g

Spinach and Feta Bread

Degree of difficulty: ★★☆☆☆
Average expense: $4-$5
Preparation time: 15 minutes
Servings: 1.5 lb loaf (12 slices)

Ingredients:

- 1 cup warm water (at a temp. around 110 deg.F)
- 2 1/4 teaspoons active dry yeast
- 3 cups whole wheat flour
- 2 tablespoons olive oil
- 1 cup severed fresh spinach
- 1/2 cup crumbled feta cheese

Directions:

1. Include warm water and yeast to the bread machine. Allow yeast to bloom for 5-10 minutes.
2. Include whole wheat flour, olive oil, severed spinach, and feta cheese to the machine.
3. Set the bread machine to the basic/normal setting and start the cycle.
4. Once baking cycle is complete, take out the Spinach and Feta Bread and allow it to relax prior to slicing.

Per serving: Calories: 160kcal; Fat: 3g; Carbs: 29g; Protein: 5g

Caprese Bread

Degree of difficulty: ★★★☆☆
Average expense: $4-$5
Preparation time: 15 minutes
Servings: 1.5 lb loaf (12 slices)

Ingredients:

- 1 cup warm water (at a temp. around 110 deg.F)
- 2 1/4 teaspoons active dry yeast
- 3 cups whole wheat flour
- 2 tablespoons olive oil
- 1/2 cup cubed tomatoes
- 1/2 cup fresh basil leaves, severed
- 1/2 cup fresh mozzarella cheese, cubed

Directions:

1. Include warm water and yeast to the bread machine. Allow yeast to bloom for 5-10 minutes.
2. Include whole wheat flour and olive oil to the machine.
3. Set the bread machine to the basic/normal setting and start the cycle.
4. Once the dough has kneaded and risen, take out it from the machine and carefully wrap in the cubed tomatoes, severed basil, and cubed mozzarella.
5. Put it back in the machine and continue baking as per to the machine's guidelines.

Per serving: Calories: 160kcal; Fat: 4g; Carbs: 26g; Protein: 5g

Bacon Cheddar Bread

Degree of difficulty: ★★★☆☆ **Average expense:** $5-$6
Preparation time: 15 minutes **Servings:** 1.5 lb loaf (12 slices)

Ingredients:

- 1 cup warm water (at a temp. around 110 deg.F)
- 2 1/4 teaspoons active dry yeast
- 3 cups whole wheat flour
- 2 tablespoons olive oil
- 1/2 cup cooked and crumbled bacon
- 1/2 cup teared up cheddar cheese

Directions:

1. Include warm water and yeast to the bread machine. Allow yeast to bloom for 5-10 minutes.
2. Include whole wheat flour and olive oil to the machine.
3. Set the bread machine to the basic/normal setting and start the cycle.
4. Once the dough has kneaded and risen, take out it from the machine and wrap in the cooked then crumbled bacon and teared up cheddar cheese.
5. Put it back in the machine and continue baking as per to the machine's guidelines.

Per serving: Calories: 170kcal; Fat: 5g; Carbs: 28g; Protein: 5g

Olive Rosemary Bread

Degree of difficulty: ★★☆☆☆ **Average expense:** $3-$4
Preparation time: 15 minutes **Servings:** 1.5 lb loaf (12 slices)

Ingredients:

- 1 cup warm water (at a temp. around 110 deg.F)
- 2 1/4 teaspoons active dry yeast
- 3 cups whole wheat flour
- 2 tablespoons olive oil
- 1/2 cup eroded and severed black or green olives
- 1 tablespoon dried rosemary

Directions:

1. Include warm water and yeast to the bread machine. Allow yeast to bloom for 5-10 minutes.
2. Include flour, olive oil, severed olives, and dried rosemary to the machine.
3. Set the bread machine to the basic/normal setting and start the cycle.
4. Once baking cycle is complete, take out the Olive Rosemary Bread and allow it to relax prior to slicing.

Per serving: Calories: 150kcal; Fat: 3g; Carbs: 28g; Protein: 4.5g

Asiago and Sun-Dried Tomato Bread

Degree of difficulty: ★★☆☆☆   **Average expense:** $4-$5

Preparation time: 15 minutes   **Servings:** 1.5 lb loaf (12 slices)

Ingredients:

- 1 cup warm water (at a temp. around 110 deg.F)
- 2 1/4 teaspoons active dry yeast
- 3 cups whole wheat flour
- 2 tablespoons olive oil
- 1/2 cup grated Asiago cheese
- 1/4 cup severed sun-dried tomatoes

Directions:

1. Include warm water and yeast to the bread machine. Allow yeast to bloom for 5-10 minutes.
2. Include whole wheat flour, olive oil, grated Asiago cheese, and severed sun-dried tomatoes to the machine.
3. Set the bread machine to the basic/normal setting and start the cycle.
4. Once baking cycle is complete, take out the Olive Rosemary Bread and allow it to relax prior to slicing.

Per serving: Calories: 160kcal; Fat: 4g; Carbs: 26g; Protein: 5g

Sweet Sensation

This chapter is a delightful journey into the world of sweet breads, where we explore the softer, sweeter side of bread-making.

Sweet breads are a special treat, often blending the lines between bread and dessert. From the classic cinnamon-raisin bread to more adventurous concoctions like blueberry-lemon bread and chocolate chip bread, each recipe has been carefully crafted for your bread machine.

Cinnamon Swirl Bread

Degree of difficulty: ★★☆☆☆ **Average expense:** $2-$3

Preparation time: 10 minutes **Servings:** 1.5 lb loaf (12 slices)

Ingredients:

- 1 cup warm water (at a temp. around 110 deg.F)
- 2 1/4 teaspoons active dry yeast
- 3 cups whole wheat flour
- 2 tablespoons honey
- 1 teaspoon salt
- 1 1/2 teaspoons ground cinnamon

Directions:

1. Include warm water and yeast to the bread machine. Allow yeast to bloom for 5-10 minutes.
2. Include whole wheat flour, honey, and salt to the pan.
3. Set the bread machine to the sweet bread setting and start the cycle.
4. Once the dough has kneaded and risen, take out it from the machine then roll it out.
5. Spray cinnamon evenly over the dough, roll it up, and place it back in the machine.
6. Continue baking as per to the machine's guidelines.

Per serving: Calories: 120kcal; Fat: 0.5g; Carbs: 25g; Protein: 4g

Cinnamon Raisin Bread

Degree of difficulty: ★★☆☆☆ **Average expense:** $3-$4

Preparation time: 10 minutes **Servings:** 1.5 lb loaf (12 slices)

Ingredients:

- 1 1/4 cups warm water (at a temp. around 110 deg.F)
- 2 1/4 teaspoons active dry yeast
- 2 1/2 cups bread flour
- 2 tablespoons honey
- 1 1/2 teaspoons cinnamon
- 1/2 teaspoon salt
- 2 tablespoons olive oil
- 1/2 cup raisins

Directions:

1. Include warm water to the bread machine's pan.
2. Spray yeast across the water and allow it to relax for around 5 minutes until it becomes frothy.
3. Include bread flour, honey, cinnamon, salt, and olive oil to the pan.
4. Put pan in the bread machine, choose the sweet bread setting and start the machine.
5. Once the machine beeps to include extras (typically after the first knead), include the raisins.
6. Once baking cycle is complete, take out the cinnamon raisin bread and allow it to relax prior to slicing.

Per serving: Calories: 150kcal; Fat: 2.5g; Carbs: 30g; Protein: 4g

Lemon Zucchini Bread

Degree of difficulty: ★★☆☆☆

Average expense: $2-$3

Preparation time: 15 minutes

Servings: 1.5 lb loaf (12 slices)

Ingredients:

- 1 cup grated zucchini (extra moisture squeezed out)
- 1/4 cup olive oil
- 2 eggs
- 1/2 cup honey
- 1 1/2 teaspoons lemon zest
- 2 tablespoons lemon juice
- 2 1/4 cups bread flour
- 1 1/2 teaspoons baking powder
- 1/2 teaspoon baking soda
- 1/2 teaspoon salt

Directions:

1. Inside a container, mix the grated zucchini, olive oil, eggs, honey, lemon zest, and lemon juice.
2. Inside an extra container, blend bread flour, baking powder, baking soda, and salt.
3. Put wet components to dry components and mix until well blended.
4. Put the batter in the bread machine, choose sweet bread setting, and start the machine.
5. Once baking cycle is complete, take out the Lemon Zucchini Bread and allow it to relax prior to slicing.

Per serving: Calories: 170kcal; Fat: 6g; Carbs: 25g; Protein: 4g

Blueberry Lemon Bread

Degree of difficulty: ★★☆☆☆

Average expense: $4-$5

Preparation time: 15 minutes

Servings: 1.5 lb loaf (12 slices)

Ingredients:

- 1 cup blueberries (fresh or frozen)
- 1/4 cup olive oil
- 2 eggs
- 1/2 cup honey
- 1 1/2 teaspoons lemon zest
- 2 tablespoons lemon juice
- 2 1/4 cups bread flour
- 1 1/2 teaspoons baking powder
- 1/2 teaspoon baking soda
- 1/2 teaspoon salt

Directions:

1. Inside a container, carefully wrap the blueberries into olive oil, eggs, honey, lemon zest, and lemon juice.
2. Inside an extra container, blend bread flour, baking powder, baking soda, and salt.
3. Put wet components to dry components and mix till well blended.
4. Put the batter in the bread machine, choose sweet bread setting, and start the machine.
5. Once baking cycle is complete, take out the Blueberry Lemon Bread and allow it to relax prior to slicing.

Per serving: Calories: 170kcal; Fat: 6g; Carbs: 26g; Protein: 4g

Sweet Potato Bread

Degree of difficulty: ★★☆☆☆
Average expense: $3-$4
Preparation time: 15 minutes
Servings: 1.5 lb loaf (12 slices)

Ingredients:

- 1 1/4 cups warm water (at a temp. around 110 deg.F)
- 2 1/4 teaspoons active dry yeast
- 2 cups bread flour
- 1 cup mashed sweet potatoes (cooled)
- 2 tablespoons honey
- 1 1/2 teaspoons salt

Directions:

1. Include warm water to the bread machine's pan.
2. Spray yeast across the water and allow it to relax for around 5 minutes until it becomes frothy.
3. Include bread flour, mashed sweet potatoes, honey, and salt to the pan.
4. Put pan in the bread machine, choose sweet bread setting and start the machine.
5. Once baking cycle is complete, take out the sweet potato bread and allow it to relax prior to slicing.

Per serving: Calories: 160kcal; Fat: 2g; Carbs: 30g; Protein: 4g

Chocolate Chip Bread

Degree of difficulty: ★★☆☆☆
Average expense: $4-$5
Preparation time: 10 minutes
Servings: 1.5 lb loaf (12 slices)

Ingredients:

- 1 cup warm milk
- 2 1/4 teaspoons active dry yeast
- 3 cups whole wheat flour
- 2 tablespoons honey
- 1/2 cup organic dark chocolate chips

Directions:

1. Include warm milk and yeast to the bread machine. Allow yeast to bloom for 5-10 minutes.
2. Include whole wheat flour, honey, and chocolate chips to the machine.
3. Set the bread machine to the sweet setting and start the cycle.
4. Once baking cycle is complete, take out the chocolate chip bread and allow it to relax prior to slicing.

Per serving: Calories: 150kcal; Fat: 2.5g; Carbs: 28g; Protein: 4g

Amish Friendship Bread

Degree of difficulty: ★★☆☆☆ **Average expense:** $3-$4

Preparation time: 15 minutes **Servings:** 1.5 lb loaf (12 slices)

Ingredients:

- 1 cup Amish Friendship Bread starter
- 2/3 cup milk
- 2 cups bread flour
- 1/2 cup sugar
- 1/2 cup oil
- 3 eggs
- 1 1/2 teaspoons baking powder
- 1/2 teaspoon baking soda
- 1/2 teaspoon salt
- 1 teaspoon vanilla extract
- 1 teaspoon cinnamon
- 1/2 cup severed nuts (optional)

Directions:

1. Inside your blending container, blend the Amish Friendship Bread starter, baking soda, salt, milk, vanilla extract, bread flour, sugar, oil, eggs, baking powder, and cinnamon.
2. If you like, include severed nuts to the batter.
3. Put the batter in the bread machine, choose the sweet bread setting, and start the machine.
4. Once baking cycle is complete, take out the Amish Friendship Bread and allow it to relax prior to slicing.

Per serving: Calories: 220kcal; Fat: 9g; Carbs: 31g; Protein: 4g

Blueberry Muffin Bread

Degree of difficulty: ★★☆☆☆
Average expense: $4-$5
Preparation time: 10 minutes
Servings: 1.5 lb loaf (12 slices)

Ingredients:

- 1 cup warm milk
- 2 1/4 teaspoons active dry yeast
- 3 cups whole wheat flour
- 2 tablespoons honey
- 1 cup fresh or frozen blueberries

Directions:

1. Include warm milk and yeast to the bread machine. Allow yeast to bloom for 5-10 minutes.
2. Include whole wheat flour, honey, and blueberries to the machine.
3. Set the bread machine to the sweet bread setting and start the cycle.
4. Once baking cycle is complete, take out the Blueberry Muffin Bread and allow it to relax prior to slicing.

Per serving: Calories: 130kcal; Fat: 1g; Carbs: 28g; Protein: 4.5g

Banana Nut Bread

Degree of difficulty: ★★☆☆☆
Average expense: $3-$4
Preparation time: 15 minutes
Servings: 1.5 lb loaf (12 slices)

Ingredients:

- 2 ripe bananas, mashed
- 2 1/4 teaspoons active dry yeast
- 3 cups whole wheat flour
- 2 tablespoons honey
- 1/2 cup severed walnuts

Directions:

1. Mash the bananas and include them to the bread machine along with yeast.
2. Include whole wheat flour, honey, and severed walnuts to the machine.
3. Set the bread machine to the sweet bread setting and start the cycle.
4. Once baking cycle is complete, take out the Banana Nut Bread and allow it to relax prior to slicing.

Per serving: Calories: 160kcal; Fat: 3g; Carbs: 30g; Protein: 4.5g

Cranberry Walnut Bread

Degree of difficulty: ★★☆☆☆

Average expense: $3-$4

Preparation time: 15 minutes

Servings: 1.5 lb loaf (12 slices)

Ingredients:

- 1 1/4 cups warm water (at a temp. around 110 deg.F)
- 2 1/4 teaspoons active dry yeast
- 3 cups bread flour
- 1/2 cup dried cranberries
- 1/2 cup severed walnuts
- 2 tablespoons honey
- 1 1/2 teaspoons salt

Directions:

1. Include warm water to the bread machine's pan.
2. Spray yeast across the water around 5 minutes until it becomes frothy.
3. Include bread flour, dried cranberries, severed walnuts, honey, and salt to the pan.
4. Put pan in the bread machine, choose the sweet bread setting, and start the machine.
5. Once baking cycle is complete, take out the Cranberry Walnut Bread and allow it to relax prior to slicing.

Per serving: Calories: 180kcal; Fat: 5g; Carbs: 30g; Protein: 5g

Almond Poppy Seed Bread

Degree of difficulty: ★★☆☆☆

Average expense: $3-$4

Preparation time: 15 minutes

Servings: 1.5 lb loaf (12 slices)

Ingredients:

- 1 cup warm milk
- 2 1/4 teaspoons active dry yeast
- 3 cups whole wheat flour
- 2 tablespoons honey
- 2 tablespoons poppy seeds
- 1/4 cup carved almonds

Directions:

1. Include warm milk and yeast to the bread machine. Allow yeast to bloom for 5-10 minutes.
2. Include whole wheat flour, honey, poppy seeds, and carved almonds to the machine.
3. Set the bread machine to the sweet bread setting and start the cycle.
4. Once baking cycle is complete, take out the Almond Poppy Seed Bread and allow it to relax prior to slicing.

Per serving: Calories: 140kcal; Fat: 3.5g; Carbs: 28g; Protein: 5g

Cranberry Orange Bread

Degree of difficulty: ★★☆☆☆ **Average expense:** $3-$4
Preparation time: 15 minutes **Servings:** 1.5 lb loaf (12 slices)

Ingredients:

- 1 cup warm water (at a temp. around 110 deg.F)
- 2 1/4 teaspoons active dry yeast
- 3 cups whole wheat flour
- 2 tablespoons honey
- 1/2 cup dried cranberries
- Zest of 1 orange

Directions:

1. Include warm water and yeast to the bread machine. Allow yeast to bloom for 5-10 minutes.
2. Include flour, honey, dried cranberries, and orange zest to the machine.
3. Set the bread machine to the sweet bread setting and start the cycle.
4. Once baking cycle is complete, take out the Cranberry Orange Bread and allow it to relax prior to slicing.

Per serving: Calories: 140kcal; Fat: 0.5g; Carbs: 30g; Protein: 4g

Nutella Swirl Bread

Degree of difficulty: ★★☆☆☆ **Average expense:** $3-$4
Preparation time: 15 minutes **Servings:** 1.5 lb loaf (12 slices)

Ingredients:

- 1 cup warm milk
- 2 1/4 teaspoons active dry yeast
- 3 cups whole wheat flour
- 2 tablespoons honey
- 1/4 cup Nutella (or other hazelnut spread)

Directions:

1. Include warm milk and yeast to the bread machine. Allow yeast to bloom for 5-10 minutes.
2. Include whole wheat flour and honey to the machine.
3. Set the bread machine to the sweet bread setting and start the cycle.
4. Once the dough has kneaded and risen, take out it from the machine then roll it out.
5. Disperse Nutella evenly over the dough, roll it up, and place it back in the machine.
6. Continue baking as per to the machine's guidelines.

Per serving: Calories: 180kcal; Fat: 3.5g; Carbs: 30g; Protein: 5g

Apple Cinnamon Bread

Degree of difficulty: ★★☆☆☆ **Average expense:** $3-$4

Preparation time: 15 minutes **Servings:** 1.5 lb loaf (12 slices)

Ingredients:

- 1 cup warm water (at a temp. around 110 deg.F)
- 2 1/4 teaspoons active dry yeast
- 3 cups whole wheat flour
- 2 tablespoons honey
- 1 cup cubed apples
- 1 1/2 teaspoons ground cinnamon

Directions:

1. Include warm water and yeast to the bread machine. Allow yeast to bloom for 5-10 minutes.
2. Include whole wheat flour, honey, cubed apples, and ground cinnamon to the machine.
3. Set the bread machine to sweet bread setting and start the cycle.
4. Once baking cycle is complete, take out the Apple Cinnamon Bread and allow it to relax prior to slicing.

Per serving: Calories: 150kcal; Fat: 1g; Carbs: 32g; Protein: 4.5g

Maple Pecan Bread

Degree of difficulty: ★★☆☆☆ **Average expense:** $4-$5

Preparation time: 15 minutes **Servings:** 1.5 lb loaf (12 slices)

Ingredients:

- 1 cup warm water (at a temp. around 110 deg.F)
- 2 1/4 teaspoons active dry yeast
- 3 cups whole wheat flour
- 2 tablespoons pure maple syrup
- 1/2 cup severed pecans

Directions:

1. Include warm water and yeast to the bread machine. Allow yeast to bloom for 5-10 minutes.
2. Include whole wheat flour, maple syrup, and severed pecans to the machine.
3. Set the bread machine to sweet bread setting and start the cycle.
4. Once baking cycle is complete, take out the Maple Pecan Bread and allow it to relax prior to slicing.

Per serving: Calories: 160kcal; Fat: 3.5g; Carbs: 29g; Protein: 4g

Fig and Walnut Bread

Degree of difficulty: ★★☆☆☆

Average expense: $4-$5

Preparation time: 15 minutes

Servings: 1.5 lb loaf (12 slices)

Ingredients:

- 1 cup warm water (at a temp. around 110 deg.F)
- 2 1/4 teaspoons active dry yeast
- 3 cups whole wheat flour
- 2 tablespoons honey
- 1/2 cup dried figs, severed
- 1/2 cup severed walnuts

Directions:

1. Include warm water and yeast to the bread machine. Allow yeast to bloom for 5-10 minutes.
2. Include whole wheat flour, honey, severed dried figs, and severed walnuts to the machine.
3. Set the bread machine to sweet bread setting and start the cycle.
4. Once baking cycle is complete, take out the Fig and Walnut Bread and allow it to relax prior to slicing.

Per serving: Calories: 160kcal; Fat: 3.5g; Carbs: 28g; Protein: 4.5g

Cherry Almond Bread

Degree of difficulty: ★★☆☆☆

Average expense: $4-$5

Preparation time: 15 minutes

Servings: 1.5 lb loaf (12 slices)

Ingredients:

- 1 cup warm water (at a temp. around 110 deg.F)
- 2 1/4 teaspoons active dry yeast
- 3 cups whole wheat flour
- 2 tablespoons honey
- 1/2 cup dried cherries
- 1/4 cup carved almonds

Directions:

1. Include warm water and yeast to the bread machine. Allow yeast to bloom for 5-10 minutes.
2. Include whole wheat flour, honey, dried cherries, and carved almonds to the machine.
3. Set the bread machine to sweet bread setting and start the cycle.
4. Once baking cycle is complete, take out the Cherry Almond Bread and allow it to relax prior to slicing.

Per serving: Calories: 140kcal; Fat: 2.5g; Carbs: 28g; Protein: 4g

Cherry Chocolate Bread

Degree of difficulty: ★★☆☆☆ **Average expense:** $5-$6

Preparation time: 15 minutes **Servings:** 1.5 lb loaf (12 slices)

Ingredients:

- 1 cup warm water (at a temp. around 110 deg.F)
- 2 1/4 teaspoons active dry yeast
- 3 cups whole wheat flour
- 2 tablespoons honey
- 1/2 cup dried cherries
- 1/4 cup organic dark chocolate chips

Directions:

1. Include warm water and yeast to the bread machine. Allow yeast to bloom for 5-10 minutes.
2. Include whole wheat flour, honey, dried cherries, and dark chocolate chips to the machine.
3. Set the bread machine to sweet bread setting and start the cycle.
4. Once baking cycle is complete, take out the Cherry Almond Bread and allow it to relax prior to slicing.

Per serving: Calories: 160kcal; Fat: 2.5g; Carbs: 32g; Protein: 4.5g

Coconut Pineapple Bread

Degree of difficulty: ★★☆☆☆ **Average expense:** $4-$5

Preparation time: 15 minutes **Servings:** 1.5 lb loaf (12 slices)

Ingredients:

- 1 cup warm water (at a temp. around 110 deg.F)
- 2 1/4 teaspoons active dry yeast
- 2 cups all-purpose flour
- 1 cup whole wheat flour
- 1/2 cup shredded coconut
- 1/2 cup crushed pineapple, drained
- 2 tablespoons honey
- 1/4 cup coconut milk
- 1/4 cup olive oil
- 1/2 teaspoon salt

Directions:

1. Add both types of flour, shredded coconut, and salt to the bread machine's pan.
2. In a separate bowl, combine warm water, honey, active dry yeast, coconut milk, and olive oil. Let it sit for 5 minutes until frothy.
3. Pour the yeast mixture into the bread machine's pan.
4. Add the crushed pineapple to the mixture.
5. Set the bread machine to the sweet bread setting.
6. Start the machine and let it run through the cycle.
7. Once the baking cycle is complete, remove the bread and let it cool before slicing.

Per serving: Calories: 190kcal; Fat: 7g; Carbs: 28g; Protein: 3.5g

Apricot Ginger Bread

Degree of difficulty: ★★☆☆☆ **Average expense:** $4-$5

Preparation time: 15 minutes **Servings:** 1.5 lb loaf (12 slices)

Ingredients:

- 1 cup warm water (at a temp. around 110 deg.F)
- 2 1/4 teaspoons active dry yeast
- 3 cups whole wheat flour
- 2 tablespoons honey
- 1/2 cup dried apricots, severed
- 2 tablespoons candied ginger, finely severed

Directions:

1. Include warm water and yeast to the bread machine. Allow yeast to bloom for 5-10 minutes.
2. Include whole wheat flour, honey, severed dried apricots, and candied ginger to the machine.
3. Set the bread machine to sweet bread setting and start the cycle.
4. Once baking cycle is complete, take out the Cherry Almond Bread and allow it to relax prior to slicing.

Per serving: Calories: 150kcal; Fat: 2g; Carbs: 30g; Protein: 4.5g

Raspberry White Chocolate Bread

Degree of difficulty: ★★☆☆☆ **Average expense:** $5-$6

Preparation time: 10 minutes **Servings:** 1.5 lb loaf (12 slices)

Ingredients:

- 1 cup warm water (at a temp. around 110 deg.F)
- 2 1/4 teaspoons active dry yeast
- 3 cups whole wheat flour
- 2 tablespoons honey
- 1/2 cup fresh or frozen raspberries
- 1/2 cup organic white chocolate chips

Directions:

1. Include warm water and yeast to the bread machine. Allow yeast to bloom for 5-10 minutes.
2. Include flour, honey, fresh or frozen raspberries, and white chocolate chips to the machine.
3. Set the bread machine to sweet bread setting and start the cycle.
4. Once baking cycle is complete, take out the Cherry Almond Bread and allow it to relax prior to slicing.

Per serving: Calories: 160kcal; Fat: 5g; Carbs: 28g; Protein: 5g

Orange Poppy Seed Bread

Degree of difficulty: ★★☆☆☆ **Average expense:** $3-$4

Preparation time: 15 minutes **Servings:** 1.5 lb loaf (12 slices)

Ingredients:

- 1 cup warm water (at a temp. around 110 deg.F)
- 2 1/4 teaspoons active dry yeast
- 3 cups bread flour
- 1/4 cup sugar
- 2 tablespoons orange zest
- 1/4 cup fresh orange juice
- 2 tablespoons poppy seeds
- 1/2 teaspoon salt
- 2 tablespoons butter, melted

Directions:

1. Add the bread flour, sugar, orange zest, poppy seeds, and salt to the bread machine's pan.
2. In a separate bowl, mix the warm water, orange juice, melted butter, and active dry yeast. Let it sit for 5 minutes until frothy.
3. Pour the yeast mixture into the bread machine's pan.
4. Set the bread machine to the sweet bread setting.
5. Start the machine and let it run through the cycle.
6. Once the baking cycle is complete, remove the bread and allow it to cool before slicing.

Per serving: Calories: 150kcal; Fat: 2.5g; Carbs: 29g; Protein: 3g

Pumpkin Chocolate Swirl Bread

Degree of difficulty: ★★☆☆☆ **Average expense:** $4-$5

Preparation time: 15 minutes **Servings:** 1.5 lb loaf (12 slices)

Ingredients:

- 1 cup warm water (at a temp. around 110 deg.F)
- 2 1/4 teaspoons active dry yeast
- 3 cups whole wheat flour
- 2 tablespoons honey
- 1/2 cup tinned pumpkin puree
- 1/4 cup organic dark chocolate chips

Directions:

1. Include warm water and yeast to the bread machine. Allow yeast to bloom for 5-10 minutes.
2. Include whole wheat flour, honey, and tinned pumpkin puree to the machine.
3. Set the bread machine to the sweet bread setting and start the cycle.
4. Once the dough has kneaded and risen, take out it from the machine then roll it out.
5. Sprinkle dark chocolate chips evenly over the dough, roll it up, and place it back in the machine.
6. Continue baking as per to the machine's guidelines.

Per serving: Calories: 160kcal; Fat: 3.5g; Carbs: 30g; Protein: 4.5g

International Bread Adventure

Bread is a universal language, understood and loved across the globe. Each country and region have its own unique bread-making traditions, ingredients, and techniques, which we have carefully captured in these recipes. From the rustic Italian Ciabatta to the savory Indian Naan, this chapter is a culinary expedition that will broaden your baking horizons.

These recipes have been adapted for your bread machine, making them accessible and easy to follow. Whether you are a novice baker or have been using a bread machine for years, these international breads will offer new challenges and delights.

Naan Bread

Degree of difficulty: ★★★☆☆ **Average expense:** $3-$4

Preparation time: 20 minutes **Servings:** 6 naans

Ingredients:

- 1 cup warm water (at a temp. around 110 deg.F)
- 2 1/4 teaspoons active dry yeast
- 2 tablespoons honey
- 1/4 cup plain yogurt
- 3 cups all-purpose flour
- 1 teaspoon salt
- 1/2 teaspoon baking powder
- 1 tablespoon olive oil

Directions:

1. Include warm water and yeast to the bread machine. Allow yeast to bloom for 5-10 minutes.
2. Include yogurt, flour, honey, salt, baking powder, and olive oil to the pan in the bread machine.
3. Select dough setting on the bread machine and let it complete its cycle.
4. Warm up a non-stick frying pan in a med-high temp.
5. Split dough into 6 equal parts then roll out each piece into a teardrop shape.
6. Cook each naan for 2-3 minutes on all sides till mildly browned and puffy.
7. Present warm.

Per serving: Calories: 215kcal; Fat: 2g; Carbs: 42g; Protein: 7g

Greek Pita Bread

Degree of difficulty: ★★★☆☆ **Average expense:** $2-$3

Preparation time: 20 minutes **Servings:** 8 pitas

Ingredients:

- 1 cup warm water (at a temp. around 110 deg.F)
- 1 ½ teaspoons active dry yeast
- 1 tablespoons honey
- 2 ½ cups whole wheat flour
- 1 teaspoon salt
- 1 tablespoon olive oil

Directions:

1. Include warm water and yeast to the bread machine. Allow yeast to bloom for 5-10 minutes.
2. Bring whole wheat flour, salt, and olive oil to the pan in the bread machine.
3. Select dough setting on the bread machine and allow it to complete its cycle.
4. Warm up the oven to 500 deg.F.
5. Split dough into 8 equal parts then roll each into a ball. Let them rest for 10 minutes.
6. Roll out each ball into a 6-inch circle.
7. Bake for 5-7 minutes, till puffed and mildly browned.
8. Present warm.

Per serving: Calories: 157kcal; Fat: 3g; Carbs: 28g; Protein: 5g

Mexican Tortilla Bread

Degree of difficulty: ★★★☆☆   **Average expense:** $2-$3

Preparation time: 20 minutes   **Servings:** 12 tortillas

Ingredients:

- 3/4 cup warm water (at a temp. around 110 deg.F)
- 2 cups all-purpose flour
- 1/2 teaspoon salt
- 3 tablespoons olive oil

Directions:

1. Put all-purpose flour, salt, olive oil and warm water to the pan in the bread machine.
2. Select dough setting on the bread machine and allow it to complete its cycle.
3. Warm up a non-stick pan in a med-high temp.
4. Split dough into 12 equal parts then roll each part into a ball.
5. Roll out each ball into a thin, flat circle.
6. Cook each tortilla for 1-2 minutes on all sides till mildly browned and mildly puffed.
7. Present warm.

Per serving: Calories: 108kcal; Fat: 4g; Carbs: 16g; Protein: 2g

Swedish Limpa Bread

Degree of difficulty: ★★☆☆ ☆

Preparation time: 10 minutes

Average expense: $4-$5

Servings: 1.5 lb loaf (12 slices)

Ingredients:

- 1 cup lukewarm water
- 2 tablespoons molasses
- 1 tablespoon olive oil
- 1 teaspoon salt
- 2 cups whole wheat flour
- 1 cup bread flour
- 1 ½ teaspoons active dry yeast
- 1 teaspoon caraway seeds
- 1 teaspoon fennel seeds

Directions:

1. Activate the yeast by combining lukewarm water, molasses, and yeast in the bread machine pan. Allow it to relax for 5-10 minutes until frothy.
2. Include olive oil, salt, whole wheat flour, bread flour, caraway seeds, and fennel seeds to the pan in the bread machine.
3. Select the whole wheat setting on the bread machine and let it complete its cycle.
4. Once done, take out the bread and allow it to relax prior to slicing.

Per serving: Calories: 140kcal; Fat: 2.5g; Carbs: 30g; Protein: 4g

Italian Ciabatta

Degree of difficulty: ★★★☆☆ **Average expense:** $2-$3

Preparation time: 20 minutes **Servings:** 1.5 lb loaf (12 slices)

Ingredients:

- 1 1/2 cups warm water (at a temp. around 110 deg.F)
- 1 1/2 teaspoons active dry yeast
- 3 1/4 cups bread flour
- 1 1/2 teaspoons salt
- 1 teaspoon sugar
- 1 tablespoon olive oil

Directions:

1. Include warm water and yeast to the bread machine. Allow yeast to bloom for 5-10 minutes.
2. Add the bread flour, salt, and olive oil to the pan.
3. Select the dough setting on your bread machine and start the cycle.
4. Once the dough cycle is complete, shape the dough into a traditional ciabatta loaf on a floured surface. Let it rise for an additional 30 minutes.
5. Preheat your oven to 425°F (220°C). Transfer the loaf to a baking sheet and bake for 25-30 minutes, until golden brown.
6. Let the ciabatta cool before slicing and serving.

Per serving: Calories: 140kcal; Fat: 1.5g; Carbs: 27g; Protein: 3g

Japanese Hokkaido Milk Bread

Degree of difficulty: ★★☆☆ ☆ **Average expense:** $3-$4

Preparation time: 10 minutes **Servings:** 1.5 lb loaf (12 slices)

Ingredients:

- 1/2 cup warm milk
- 1 1/2 teaspoons active dry yeast
- 2 tablespoons sugar
- 2 1/4 cups bread flour
- 1 teaspoon salt
- 2 tablespoons butter

Directions:

1. Activate the yeast by combining warm milk and sugar in the bread machine pan. Include the yeast and allow it to relax for 5-10 minutes until frothy.
2. Include bread flour, salt, and butter to the pan in the bread machine.
3. Select the basic/normal setting on the bread machine and let it complete its cycle.
4. Once done, let the bread cool prior to slicing.

Per serving: Calories: 120kcal; Fat: 2g; Carbs: 22g; Protein: 4g

Russian Borodinsky Bread

Degree of difficulty: ★★☆☆☆ **Average expense:** $4-$5

Preparation time: 10 minutes **Servings:** 1.5 lb loaf (12 slices)

Ingredients:

- 1 cup warm water (at a temp. around 110 deg.F)
- 1 1/2 teaspoons active dry yeast
- 2 tablespoons molasses
- 2 teaspoons caraway seeds
- 1 1/2 cups rye flour
- 1 1/2 cups bread flour
- 1 teaspoon salt

Directions:

1. Activate the yeast by combining warm water, molasses, and yeast in the bread machine pan. Allow it to relax for 5-10 minutes until frothy.
2. Include caraway seeds, rye flour, bread flour, and salt to the pan in the bread machine.
3. Select the whole wheat bread setting on the bread machine and let it complete its cycle.
4. Let the bread cool prior to slicing.

Per serving: Calories: 150kcal; Fat: 3g; Carbs: 29g; Protein: 5g

Cuban Bread

Degree of difficulty: ★★★☆☆

Average expense: $4-$5

Preparation time: 15 minutes

Servings: 1.5 lb loaf (12 slices)

Ingredients:

- 1 cup warm water (at a temp. around 110 deg.F)
- 1 1/2 teaspoons active dry yeast
- 2 teaspoons honey
- 3 cups bread flour
- 1 1/2 teaspoons salt
- 2 tablespoons of high-quality lard

Directions:

1. Activate the yeast by combining warm water and honey in the bread machine pan. Include the yeast and allow it to relax for 5-10 minutes until frothy.
2. Melt the lard in a microwave.
3. Bring bread flour, salt, melted lard and olive oil to the pan in the bread machine.
4. Select the basic/normal setting on the bread machine and let it complete its cycle.
5. Once done, let the bread cool prior to slicing.

Per serving: Calories: 140kcal; Fat: 7g; Carbs: 22g; Protein: 4g

Irish Brown Bread

Degree of difficulty: ★★☆☆☆

Average expense: $2-$3

Preparation time: 10 minutes

Servings: 1.5 lb loaf (12 slices)

Ingredients:

- 1 1/2 cups whole wheat flour
- 1 1/2 cups all-purpose flour
- 1 teaspoon salt
- 1 teaspoon baking soda
- 1 1/2 cups buttermilk

Directions:

1. Blend whole wheat flour, all-purpose flour, salt, and baking soda in the bread machine pan.
2. Include buttermilk to the pan.
3. Select whole wheat setting on the bread machine and let it complete its cycle.
4. Let the bread cool prior to slicing.

Per serving: Calories: 98kcal; Fat: 1g; Carbs: 17g; Protein: 3g

Indian Roti

Degree of difficulty: ★★★☆☆ **Average expense:** $1-$2

Preparation time: 20 minutes **Servings:** 8 rotis

Ingredients:

- 1 cup water (adjust as needed to get a soft dough)
- 2 cups whole wheat flour
- 1/2 teaspoon salt
- 1 1/2 cups olive oil

Directions:

1. Add the water, olive oil and salt to the bread machine's pan.
2. Gradually add the whole wheat flour to the pan.
3. Select the dough setting on your bread machine and start the cycle.
4. Split dough into 8 equal parts then roll each part into a ball.
5. Roll out each ball into a thin, flat circle.
6. Warm a griddle or skillet in a med-high temp.
7. Cook each roti for around 1 min on all sides, or till it puffs up and has brown spots.
8. Present warm.

Per serving: Calories: 120kcal; Fat: 1g; Carbs: 24g; Protein: 2g

Ethiopian Injera

Degree of difficulty: ★★★☆☆
Average expense: $5-$6
Preparation time: 20 minutes
Servings: 8 injera

Ingredients:

- 2 cups water
- 1 cup teff flour
- 1 cup all-purpose flour
- 1/2 teaspoon baking soda
- 1 teaspoon salt

Directions:

1. Inside big mixing container, blend teff flour, all-purpose flour, baking soda, and salt.
2. Slowly include water while stirring to form a smooth batter and put inside the pan.
3. Select the dough setting on your bread machine and start the cycle.
4. Warm up a non-stick griddle or injera pan in a middling temp.
5. Put a ladle of the batter onto the griddle, quickly swirling to disperse it finely like a crepe.
6. Cook for around 1-2 minutes until the edges lift, and the injera is set.
7. Take out and allow it to relax. Repeat with the rest of the batter.

Per serving: Calories: 140kcal; Fat: 1g; Carbs: 29g; Protein: 4g

Portuguese Cornbread

Degree of difficulty: ★★☆☆☆
Average expense: $3-$4
Preparation time: 10 minutes
Servings: 1.5 lb loaf (12 slices)

Ingredients:

- 1 1/2 cups cornmeal
- 1 cup all-purpose flour
- 1 1/2 teaspoons baking powder
- 1/2 teaspoon salt
- 2 tablespoons olive oil
- 1 1/4 cups water

Directions:

1. Blend cornmeal, all-purpose flour, baking powder, and salt in the bread machine pan.
2. Include olive oil and water to the pan.
3. Select the basic/normal bread setting on the bread machine and let it complete its cycle.
4. Let the cornbread cool prior to slicing.

Per serving: Calories: 110kcal; Fat: 3g; Carbs: 18g; Protein: 2g

Norwegian Kringle Bread

Degree of difficulty: ★★★☆☆　　**Average expense:** $3-$4

Preparation time: 20 minutes　　**Servings:** 1.5 lb loaf (12 slices)

Ingredients:

- 1/2 cup milk
- 1 1/2 teaspoons active dry yeast
- 2 cups all-purpose flour
- 1/2 cup sugar
- 1/2 teaspoon cardamom
- 1/2 teaspoon salt
- 1/2 cup butter, softened

Directions:

1. Activate the yeast by combining milk and yeast in the bread machine pan. Allow it to relax for 5-10 minutes until frothy.
2. Include flour, sugar, cardamom, salt, and softened butter to the pan in the bread machine.
3. Select dough setting on the bread machine and let it complete its cycle.
4. Roll out the dough into a rectangle and shape it into a ring or oval.
5. Bake at 375 deg.F for 25 minutes until golden brown.
6. Let it cool prior to presenting.

Per serving: Calories: 250kcal; Fat: 11g; Carbs: 33g; Protein: 4g

Armenian Lavash Bread

Degree of difficulty: ★★★☆☆ **Average expense:** $1-$2

Preparation time: 20 minutes **Servings:** 4 lavash

Ingredients:

- 2 cups all-purpose flour
- 1/2 teaspoon salt
- 3/4 cup water

Directions:

1. Blend all-purpose flour and salt in the bread machine pan.
2. Include water to the pan.
3. Select dough setting on the bread machine and let it complete its cycle.
4. Split dough into 4-6 equal parts then roll each into a ball.
5. Roll out each ball into a thin, flat circle.
6. Cook each lavash in a dry griddle in a med-high temp. for around 1-2 minutes on all sides.
7. Present warm.

Per serving: Calories: 100kcal; Fat: 0.5g; Carbs: 25g; Protein: 3g

Moroccan Khobz Bread

Degree of difficulty: ★★★☆☆ **Average expense:** $2-$3

Preparation time: 20 minutes **Servings:** 1.5 lb loaf (12 slices)

Ingredients:

- 1 cup warm water (at a temp. around 110 deg.F)
- 1 1/2 teaspoons active dry yeast
- 2 cups all-purpose flour
- 1 teaspoon salt
- 1 teaspoon sugar

Directions:

1. Activate the yeast by combining active dry yeast, warm water and sugar in the bread machine pan. Allow it to relax for 5-10 minutes until frothy.
2. Include all-purpose flour and salt to the pan in the bread machine.
3. Select dough setting on the bread machine and let it complete its cycle.
4. Shape the dough into big round loaf.
5. Put it on a oiled baking sheet then let it rise for 15-20 minutes.
6. Warm up oven to 375 deg.F then bake the bread for around 20-25 minutes until golden brown.
7. Let it cool prior to slicing.

Per serving: Calories: 130kcal; Fat: 0.5g; Carbs: 28g; Protein: 4g

Turkish Pide Bread

Degree of difficulty: ★★★☆☆ **Average expense:** $2-$3

Preparation time: 20 minutes **Servings:** 2 oval loaves (12 slices each)

Ingredients:

- 1 cup warm water (at a temp. around 110 deg.F)
- 2 1/4 teaspoons active dry yeast
- 3 cups all-purpose flour
- 1 teaspoon sugar
- 1 teaspoon salt
- 2 tablespoons olive oil
- 1 egg, whisked (for egg wash)

Directions:

1. Inside a container, activate the yeast by combining active dry yeast, warm water and sugar. Allow it to relax for 5-10 minutes until frothy.
2. In the bread machine, include the yeast solution, all-purpose flour, salt, and olive oil.
3. Select dough setting on the bread machine and let it complete its cycle.
4. Warm up the oven to 450 deg.F.
5. Split dough into 2 equal parts. Roll each part into an oval shape.
6. Put the ovals on a baking sheet, brush with whisked egg, and make indentations with your fingertips.
7. Bake for around 15-20 minutes until golden brown.

Per serving: Calories: 150kcal; Fat: 2.5g; Carbs: 27g; Protein: 5g

Brazilian Pao de Queijo

Degree of difficulty: ★★★☆☆

Average expense: $4-$

Preparation time: 20 minutes

Servings: 24 pieces

Ingredients:

- 1 cup milk, warmed to 110 deg.F
- 1/4 cup water, warmed to 110 deg.F
- 1/4 cup unsalted butter, melted
- 2 cups tapioca flour
- 1 teaspoon salt
- 2 large eggs
- 1 1/2 cups grated Parmesan cheese

Directions:

1. Add warm milk, water, and melted butter to the bread machine pan.
2. Over this, add the tapioca flour and salt.
3. Start the bread machine on the dough setting.
4. Once the mixture starts to combine, add the eggs and grated Parmesan cheese.
5. After the dough cycle is complete, preheat the oven to 375°F (190°C).
6. Grease a mini muffin pan. Using a spoon, portion out the dough and place it into the muffin cups.
7. Bake for 15-20 minutes until the puffs are golden and slightly crisp.

Per serving: Calories: 100kcal; Fat: 4.5g; Carbs: 11g; Protein: 2.5g

Peruvian Pan de Chancay

Degree of difficulty: ★★★☆☆ **Average expense:** $3-$4

Preparation time: 20 minutes **Servings:** 12 rolls

Ingredients:

- 1 cup warm milk
- 2 1/4 teaspoons active dry yeast
- 3 cups all-purpose flour
- 1/4 cup sugar
- 1/2 teaspoon salt
- 2 tablespoons unsalted butter, softened
- 2 large egg yolks
- 1/2 teaspoon anise seeds (optional)

Directions:

1. Add the warm milk to the bread machine's pan. Sprinkle the yeast over the milk and let it sit for about 5 minutes until frothy.
2. Add the all-purpose flour, sugar, salt, softened butter, egg yolks, and anise seeds (if using) to the pan.
3. Select dough setting on your bread machine and start the cycle.
4. Once the dough cycle is complete, divide it into small equal portions. Shape each into a round roll.
5. Place the rolls on a baking sheet, cover them, and let them rise in a warm place for about 30 minutes.
6. Preheat your oven to 350°F (175°C). Bake the rolls for about 15-20 minutes or until they turn golden brown.
7. Let the Pan de Chancay cool before serving.

Per serving: Calories: 156kcal; Fat: 3g; Carbs: 28g; Protein: 3.5g

German Pretzel Bread

Degree of difficulty: ★★★☆☆

Average expense: $3-$4

Preparation time: 25 minutes

Servings: 6 pretzel rolls

Ingredients:

- 1 1/2 cups warm water (at a temp. around 110 deg.F)
- 2 1/4 teaspoons active dry yeast
- 1 tablespoon sugar
- 3 cups bread flour
- 1 teaspoon salt
- 2/3 cup baking soda
- Coarse sea salt (for topping)

Directions:

1. Activate the yeast by combining active dry yeast, warm water and sugar in the bread machine pan. Include the yeast and allow it to relax for 5-10 minutes until frothy.
2. Include bread flour and salt to the pan in the bread machine.
3. Select dough setting on the bread machine and let it complete its cycle.
4. Warm up the oven to 475 deg.F then bring a big pot of water to a boil. Stir in the baking soda.
5. Split dough into 6 equal parts and shape them into pretzel rolls.
6. Boil each roll in the baking soda water for 30 seconds.
7. Put them on a baking sheet, spray with coarse sea salt, then bake for around 12-15 minutes until golden brown.

Per serving: Calories: 285kcal; Fat: 1g; Carbs: 59g; Protein: 8g

Argentinian Empanada Bread

Degree of difficulty: ★★★☆☆ **Average expense:** $3-$4

Preparation time: 15 minutes **Servings:** 12 empanada discs

Ingredients:

- 3 cups all-purpose flour
- 1 teaspoon salt
- 1/2 cup butter or lard
- 1/2 cup warm water (at a temp. around 110 deg.F)
- 1 egg (for egg wash)

Directions:

1. In the bread machine, blend all-purpose flour and salt.
2. Include butter or lard to the pan.
3. Choose the dough bread setting and slowly include warm water while the machine is running till a smooth dough forms.
4. Split dough into 12 equal parts then roll each into a ball.
5. Roll out each ball into a thin, flat circle.
6. Use the empanada discs to make your favorite empanada fillings, wrap them over, and seal the edges.
7. Brush the tops with whisked egg then bake at 350 deg.F for around 20 minutes until golden brown.

Per serving: Calories: 190kcal; Fat: 8g; Carbs: 24g; Protein: 4g

Jewish Challah

Degree of difficulty: ★★★☆☆   **Average expense:** $3-$4

Preparation time: 20 minutes   **Servings:** 1.5 lb loaf (12 slices)

Ingredients:

- 1/2 cup warm water (at a temp. around 110 deg.F)
- 2 1/4 teaspoons active dry yeast
- 3 cups bread flour
- 1/4 cup honey
- 2 beaten eggs
- 1/4 cup olive oil
- 1 1/2 teaspoons salt
- 1 egg yolk (for egg wash)

Directions:

1. Include warm water to the bread machine's pan.
2. Spray yeast across the water for around 5 minutes until it becomes frothy.
3. Include bread flour, honey, beaten eggs, olive oil, and salt to the pan.
4. Put pan in the bread machine, choose the dough bread setting and start the machine.
5. Once the bread machine's cycle is done, take out the dough from the pan then and place it on a mildly floured surface. Punch down the dough to take out any air bubbles and divide it into three equal portions for a simple three-strand braid or six equal portions for a more intricate six-strand braid.
6. Roll each portion into a rope of equal length, approximately 16-20 inches long.
7. If you are doing a three-strand braid, simply braid the ropes together, starting from the center and working your way towards the ends. Tweak the ends together to seal the braid.
8. If you are doing a six-strand braid, align three ropes next to each other and tweak them together at the top. Now, take the right rope and pass it over the center rope, then under the left rope. Next, take the left rope and pass it over the center rope, then under the right rope. Repeat this process till you reach the end of the ropes and tweak the ends together.
9. Put the braided Challah on your baking sheet covered with parchment paper or mildly oiled. It should now have its distinctive braid shape.
10. Brush the Challah with the egg yolk wash.
11. Allow the Challah to rise for around 30 minutes. It should become noticeably puffy during this time.
12. Warm up your oven to 350 deg. F.
13. Once the Challah has risen, put it inside the warmed up oven then bake for around 30-35 minutes or until it turns a beautiful golden brown and sounds hollow when tapped on the bottom.

Per serving: Calories: 200kcal; Fat: 6g; Carbs: 32g; Protein: 6g

Diet-Specific Bread

In this chapter, we explore a diverse selection of diet-specific bread recipes tailored to various dietary needs and preferences. Whether you are following a gluten-free, low-carb vegan or other specialized diets, these carefully curated recipes offer flavorful alternatives that cater to specific nutritional requirements, ensuring that everyone can indulge in the joy of freshly baked bread regardless of their dietary restrictions.

Gluten-free Bread

Degree of difficulty: ★★☆☆☆

Average expense: $4-$5

Preparation time: 10 minutes

Servings: 1.5 lb loaf (12 slices)

Ingredients:

- 1 1/4 cups warm water (at a temp. around 110 deg.F)
- 2 1/4 teaspoon active dry yeast
- 1 1/2 cups gluten-free flour blend
- 1 1/2 teaspoon xanthan gum
- 2 tablespoons honey
- 2 tablespoons olive oil
- 1/2 teaspoon salt

Directions:

1. Put warm water and honey to the bread machine pan. Stir to dissolve the honey.
2. Spray yeast across the water and allow it to relax for around 5-10 minutes until it becomes foamy.
3. Include the gluten-free flour blend, xanthan gum, olive oil, and salt to the pan.
4. Select gluten-free setting on your bread machine and start.
5. Once the cycle is complete, allow the bread to cool prior to slicing.

Per serving: Calories: 110kcal; Fat: 3g; Carbs: 20g; Protein: 2g

Low-Carb Almond Bread

Degree of difficulty: ★★★☆☆ **Average expense:** $6-$7

Preparation time: 20 minutes **Servings:** 1.5 lb loaf (12 slices)

Ingredients:

- 1 1/2 cups warm water (at a temp. around 110 deg.F)
- 2 1/4 teaspoons active dry yeast
- 2 1/2 cups almond flour
- 1/2 cup coconut flour
- 3 tablespoons ground flaxseed
- 2 tablespoons olive oil
- 1 teaspoon baking powder
- 1/2 teaspoon salt
- 2 eggs

Directions:

6. In the bread machine pan, combine the warm water and active dry yeast. Let it sit for about 5 minutes until frothy.
7. Add the almond flour, coconut flour, ground flaxseed, olive oil, baking powder, salt, and eggs to the pan.
8. Select the dough setting on your bread machine and start the cycle.
9. Once the dough cycle is complete, shape the dough (it will be more batter-like than traditional bread dough) in a greased bread loaf pan.
10. Allow the dough to rest and rise in a warm place for about 30 minutes.
11. Preheat your oven to 350°F (175°C). Bake the bread for about 30-35 minutes or until a toothpick inserted in the center comes out clean.
12. Let the bread cool before slicing.

Per serving: Calories: 175kcal; Fat: 14g; Carbs: 8g; Protein: 7g

Vegan Black Sesame and Matcha Swirl Bread

Degree of difficulty: ★★★☆☆ **Average expense:** $4-$5

Preparation time: 25 minutes **Servings:** 1.5 lb loaf (12 slices)

Ingredients:

- 1 1/4 cups warm water (at a temp. around 110 deg.F)
- 2 1/4 teaspoons active dry yeast
- 2 1/2 cups all-purpose flour
- 1 cup whole wheat flour
- 2 tablespoons sugar
- 1/2 teaspoon salt
- 3 tablespoons vegetable oil
- 2 tablespoons black sesame paste (can be found in Asian markets)
- 1 tablespoon matcha green tea powder

Directions:

13. In the bread machine pan, add the warm water. Sprinkle the yeast and sugar over the water and let it sit for about 5 minutes until frothy.
14. Add the all-purpose flour, whole wheat flour, salt, and vegetable oil to the pan.
15. Select the dough setting on your bread machine and start the cycle.
16. Once the dough cycle is complete, remove the dough and divide it into two equal portions.
17. Roll out one portion into a rectangle. Spread the black sesame paste evenly over the dough.
18. Roll out the second portion of dough. Sprinkle the matcha powder evenly over it.
19. Place the matcha dough on top of the sesame dough. Roll the layered dough into a log, starting from the long edge.
20. Place the dough log into a greased loaf pan with the seam side down.
21. Cover the pan and let the dough rise in a warm place for about 30-40 minutes.
22. Preheat your oven to 350°F (175°C). Bake the bread for about 30-35 minutes, or until the top is golden and a toothpick inserted into the center comes out clean.
23. Let the bread cool before slicing.

Per serving: Calories: 190kcal; Fat: 5g; Carbs: 32g; Protein: 5g

Keto Seed Bread

Degree of difficulty: ★★☆☆☆
Average expense: $5-$6
Preparation time: 10 minutes
Servings: 1.5 lb loaf (12 slices)

Ingredients:

- 1 1/2 cups almond flour
- 1/4 cup ground flaxseed
- 1/4 cup chia seeds
- 1/4 cup sunflower seeds
- 1/4 cup pumpkin seeds
- 2 teaspoon baking powder
- 4 big eggs
- 2 tablespoons olive oil
- 1/2 teaspoon salt

Directions:

1. Inside the bread machine pot, include almond flour, flaxseed, chia seeds, sunflower seeds, pumpkin seeds, baking powder, and salt.
2. Inside distinct container, whisk collectively eggs and olive oil.
3. Pour the wet solution into the bread machine pan.
4. Select the basic/normal bread setting on your bread machine and start.
5. Allow the bread to cool prior to slicing.

Per serving: Calories: 120kcal; Fat: 10g; Carbs: 5g; Protein: 6g

Paleo Coconut Bread

Degree of difficulty: ★★☆☆☆ **Average expense:** $6-$7

Preparation time: 10 minutes **Servings:** 1.5 lb loaf (12 slices)

Ingredients:

- 1 1/2 cups almond flour
- 1/2 cup coconut flour
- 1/4 cup teared up coconut
- 1 teaspoon baking soda
- 4 big eggs
- 2 tablespoons coconut oil
- 1/4 cup honey
- 1/2 teaspoon salt

Directions:

1. Inside the bread machine pot, include almond flour, coconut flour, teared up coconut, baking soda, and salt.
2. Inside distinct container, whisk collectively eggs, coconut oil, and honey.
3. Pour the wet solution into the bread machine pan.
4. Select the basic or gluten-free bread setting on your bread machine and start.
5. Allow the bread to cool prior to slicing.

Per serving: Calories: 130kcal; Fat: 9g; Carbs: 8g; Protein: 5g

Low-Fat Oat Bread

Degree of difficulty: ★★☆☆☆
Average expense: $3-$4
Preparation time: 10 minutes
Servings: 1.5 lb loaf (12 slices)

Ingredients:

- 1 1/4 cups warm water (at a temp. around 110 deg.F)
- 2 1/2 cups whole wheat flour
- 2 1/4 teaspoons active dry yeast
- 1/2 cup rolled oats
- 1 tablespoon honey
- 1/2 teaspoon salt

Directions:

1. Inside the bread machine pot, include warm water and honey.
2. Spray yeast across the water and allow it to relax for around 10 minutes until it becomes foamy.
3. Include whole wheat flour, rolled oats, and salt to the pan.
4. Select the whole wheat bread setting on your bread machine and start.
5. Allow the bread to cool prior to slicing.

Per serving: Calories: 110kcal; Fat: 1g; Carbs: 22g; Protein: 4g

High-Fiber Avocado and Oat Bran Bread

Degree of difficulty: ★★☆☆☆ **Average expense:** $4-$5
Preparation time: 10 minutes **Servings:** 1.5 lb loaf (12 slices)

Ingredients:

- 1 1/4 cups warm water (at a temp. around 110 deg.F)
- 2 1/4 teaspoons active dry yeast
- 1 ripe avocado, mashed
- 2 cups whole wheat flour
- 1 cup oat bran
- 2 tablespoons honey
- 2 tablespoons olive oil
- 1/2 teaspoon salt
- 1/4 cup ground flaxseeds
- 1/4 cup sunflower seeds

Directions:

1. In the bread machine pan, combine the warm water and yeast. Let it sit for about 5 minutes until frothy.
2. Add the mashed avocado, whole wheat flour, oat bran, honey, olive oil, salt, ground flaxseeds, and sunflower seeds to the pan.
3. Select the whole wheat bread setting on your bread machine to accommodate the denser ingredients.
4. Start the machine and let it run through the cycle.
5. Once the baking cycle is complete, remove the bread and let it cool before slicing.

Per serving: Calories: 160kcal; Fat: 8g; Carbs: 25g; Protein: 5g

Diabetic-Friendly Cinnamon Bread

Degree of difficulty: ★★☆☆☆

Average expense: $2-$

Preparation time: 10 minutes

Servings: 1.5 lb loaf (12 slices)

Ingredients:

- 1 1/4 cups warm water (at a temp. around 110 deg.F)
- 2 1/2 cups whole wheat flour
- 2 1/4 teaspoon active dry yeast
- 2 tablespoon olive oil
- 1/2 teaspoon ground cinnamon
- 1/4 teaspoon stevia
- 1/2 teaspoon salt

Directions:

1. Inside the bread machine pot, include warm water and olive oil.
2. Spray yeast across the water and allow it to relax for around 10 minutes until it becomes foamy.
3. Include whole wheat flour, ground cinnamon, stevia, and salt to the pan.
4. Select the whole wheat bread setting on your bread machine and start.
5. Allow the bread to cool prior to slicing.

Per serving: Calories: 110kcal; Fat: 3g; Carbs: 18g; Protein: 4g

Low-Sodium Apple Cinnamon Bread

Degree of difficulty: ★★☆☆☆   **Average expense:** $3-$4

Preparation time: 10 minutes   **Servings:** 1.5 lb loaf (12 slices)

Ingredients:

- 1 1/4 cups warm water (at a temp. around 110 deg.F)
- 2 1/4 teaspoons active dry yeast
- 2 cups all-purpose flour
- 1 cup whole wheat flour
- 2 tablespoons unsweetened applesauce (as a natural sweetener)
- 1 large apple, peeled and finely chopped
- 2 tablespoons honey or maple syrup
- 1/2 teaspoon cinnamon
- 1/4 teaspoon nutmeg
- 1 tablespoon olive oil

Directions:

6. Add the warm water to the bread machine's pan. Sprinkle the yeast over the water and let it sit for about 5 minutes until frothy.
7. Add the all-purpose flour, whole wheat flour, applesauce, chopped apple, honey (or maple syrup), cinnamon, nutmeg and olive oil to the pan.
8. Select the whole wheat bread setting on your bread machine to accommodate the denser ingredients.
9. Start the machine and let it run through the cycle.
10. Once the baking cycle is complete, remove the bread and let it cool before slicing.

Per serving: Calories: 135kcal; Fat: 1.5g; Carbs: 28g; Protein: 3.5g

Low-Calorie Vegetable Bread

Degree of difficulty: ★★☆☆☆ **Average expense:** $3-$4
Preparation time: 1 minutes **Servings:** 1.5 lb loaf (12 slices)

Ingredients:

- 1 1/4 cups warm water (at a temp. around 110 deg.F)
- 2 teaspoon active dry yeast
- 1 1/2 cups whole wheat flour
- 1/2 cup grated organic zucchini
- 1/2 cup grated organic carrot
- 2 tablespoon olive oil
- 1/2 teaspoon salt

Directions:

1. Inside the bread machine pot, include warm water and olive oil.
2. Spray yeast across the water and allow it to relax for around 10 minutes until it becomes foamy.
3. Include whole wheat flour, grated zucchini, grated carrot, and salt to the pan.
4. Select the whole wheat bread setting on your bread machine and start.
5. Allow the bread to cool prior to slicing.

Per serving: Calories: 120kcal; Fat: 3.5g; Carbs: 20g; Protein: 4g

High-Protein Quinoa Bread

Degree of difficulty: ★★☆☆☆ **Average expense:** $4-$5
Preparation time: 10 minutes **Servings:** 1.5 lb loaf (12 slices)

Ingredients:

- 1 1/4 cups warm water (at a temp. around 110 deg.F)
- 2 teaspoons active dry yeast
- 1 1/2 cups quinoa flour
- 1/2 cup whole wheat flour
- 2 tablespoons olive oil
- 1/2 teaspoon salt

Directions:

1. Inside the bread machine pot, include warm water and olive oil.
2. Spray yeast across the water and allow it to relax for around 10 minutes until it becomes foamy.
3. Include quinoa flour, whole wheat flour, and salt to the pan.
4. Select the whole wheat bread setting on your bread machine and start.
5. Allow the bread to cool prior to slicing.

Per serving: Calories: 120kcal; Fat: 3g; Carbs: 20g; Protein: 4g

Nut-Free Sunflower Bread

Degree of difficulty: ★★☆☆☆ **Average expense:** $4-$5

Preparation time: 10 minutes **Servings:** 1.5 lb loaf (12 slices)

Ingredients:

- 1 1/4 cups warm water (at a temp. around 110 deg.F)
- 2 teaspoons active dry yeast
- 1 1/2 cups sunflower seed flour
- 1/2 cup whole wheat flour
- 2 tablespoons olive oil
- 1/2 teaspoon salt

Directions:

1. Inside the bread machine pot, include warm water and olive oil.
2. Spray yeast across the water and allow it to relax for around 10 minutes until it becomes foamy.
3. Include sunflower seed flour, whole wheat flour, and salt to the pan.
4. Select the whole wheat bread setting on your bread machine and start.
5. Allow the bread to cool prior to slicing.

Per serving: Calories: 130kcal; Fat: 5g; Carbs: 18g; Protein: 4g

Soy-Free Tofu Bread

Degree of difficulty: ★★☆☆☆ **Average expense:** $4-$5

Preparation time: 15 minutes **Servings:** 1.5 lb loaf (12 slices)

Ingredients:

- 1 1/4 cups warm water (at a temp. around 110 deg.F)
- 2 teaspoons active dry yeast
- 1 1/2 cups rice flour
- 1/2 cup mashed silken tofu
- 2 tablespoons olive oil
- 1/2 teaspoon salt

Directions:

1. Inside the bread machine pot, include warm water and olive oil.
2. Spray yeast across the water and allow it to relax for around 10 minutes until it becomes foamy.
3. Include rice flour, mashed silken tofu, and salt to the pan.
4. Select the basic/normal bread setting on your bread machine and start.
5. Allow the bread to cool prior to slicing.

Per serving: Calories: 140kcal; Fat: 4g; Carbs: 22g; Protein: 4g

Rice Flour Shokupan Bread

Degree of difficulty: ★★☆☆☆　　**Average expense:** $5-$6

Preparation time: 15 minutes　　**Servings:** 1.5 lb loaf (12 slices)

Ingredients:

- 1 1/4 cups warm milk (at a temp. around 110 deg.F)
- 2 1/4 teaspoons active dry yeast
- 3 cups rice flour
- 2 tablespoons sugar
- 1/2 teaspoon salt
- 2 large eggs, beaten
- 3 tablespoons unsalted butter, melted
- 1/4 cup additional milk for adjusting dough consistency

Directions:

1. Add the warm milk to the bread machine pan. Sprinkle the yeast and sugar over the milk and let it sit for about 5 minutes until frothy.
2. Add the rice flour and salt to the pan.
3. Pour in the beaten eggs and melted butter.
4. Start the bread machine on the Gluten-free setting and start the machine.
5. As the machine begins to mix the ingredients, check the dough's consistency. It should be a bit stickier than regular wheat dough. If it seems too dry, gradually add the additional milk until the desired consistency is achieved.
6. Let the machine complete the cycle.
7. Once the baking cycle is complete, remove the bread and allow it to cool before slicing.

Per serving: Calories: 170kcal; Fat: 5.5g; Carbs: 28g; Protein: 4g

No-Sugar Added Fruit Bread

Degree of difficulty: ★★☆☆☆ **Average expense:** $4-$5

Preparation time: 10 minutes **Servings:** 1.5 lb loaf (12 slices)

Ingredients:

- 1 1/4 cups warm water (at a temp. around 110 deg.F)
- 2 teaspoons active dry yeast
- 1 1/2 cups whole wheat flour
- 1/2 cup dried fruit (e.g., raisins, apricots)
- 2 tablespoons olive oil
- 1/2 teaspoon cinnamon (elective)
- 1/2 teaspoon salt

Directions:

1. Inside the bread machine pot, include warm water and olive oil.
2. Spray yeast across the water and allow it to relax for around 10 minutes until it becomes foamy.
3. Include whole wheat flour, dried fruit, cinnamon (if using), and salt to the pan.
4. Select the whole wheat bread setting on your bread machine and start.
5. Allow the bread to cool prior to slicing.

Per serving: Calories: 120kcal; Fat: 3g; Carbs: 22g; Protein: 4g

Heart-Healthy Oat Bran Bread

Degree of difficulty: ★★☆☆☆ **Average expense:** $3-$4

Preparation time: 10 minutes **Servings:** 1.5 lb loaf (12 slices)

Ingredients:

- 1 1/4 cups warm water (at a temp. around 110 deg.F)
- 2 teaspoons active dry yeast
- 1 1/2 cups oat bran
- 1/2 cup whole wheat flour
- 2 tablespoons olive oil
- 1/2 teaspoon salt

Directions:

1. Inside the bread machine pot, include warm water and olive oil.
2. Spray yeast across the water and allow it to relax for around 10 minutes until it becomes foamy.
3. Include oat bran, whole wheat flour, and salt to the pan.
4. Select the whole wheat bread setting on your bread machine and start.
5. Allow the bread to cool prior to slicing.

Per serving: Calories: 110kcal; Fat: 3g; Carbs: 20g; Protein: 4g

Lactose-Free Potato Bread

Degree of difficulty: ★★☆☆ **Average expense:** $4-$5

Preparation time: 15 minutes **Servings:** 1.5 lb loaf (12 slices)

Ingredients:

- 1 1/4 cups warm water (at a temp. around 110 deg.F)
- 2 teaspoons active dry yeast
- 1 1/2 cups mashed potatoes
- 1/2 cup rice flour
- 2 tablespoons olive oil
- 1/2 teaspoon salt

Directions:

1. Inside the bread machine pot, include warm water and olive oil.
2. Spray yeast across the water and allow it to relax for around 10 minutes until it becomes foamy.
3. Include mashed potatoes, rice flour, and salt to the pan.
4. Select the gluten-free setting on your bread machine and start.
5. Allow the bread to cool prior to slicing.

Per serving: Calories: 120kcal; Fat: 3g; Carbs: 20g; Protein: 3g

Candida-Friendly Coconut Flour Bread

Degree of difficulty: ★★☆☆☆ **Average expense:** $6-$7

Preparation time: 15 minutes **Servings:** 1.5 lb loaf (12 slices)

Ingredients:

- 1/2 cups warm water (at a temp. around 110 deg.F)
- 2 1/4 teaspoons of a candida-friendly yeast alternative (such as baking soda mixed with lemon juice)
- 3 cups coconut flour
- 1/2 cup ground flaxseeds
- 1/4 cup olive oil
- 4 large eggs
- 1/2 teaspoon salt
- 1 teaspoon apple cider vinegar (helps to activate the baking soda)

Directions:

1. In a bowl, mix the warm water, olive oil, eggs, and apple cider vinegar.
2. If using baking soda as a yeast alternative, combine it with an equal part of lemon juice. This mixture should fizz and bubble, indicating it's active.
3. In the bread machine pan, combine the coconut flour, ground flaxseeds, and salt.
4. Pour the wet ingredients into the pan over the dry ingredients. Add the baking soda and lemon juice mixture last.
5. Select the gluten-free setting on your bread machine since coconut flour doesn't contain gluten and requires different handling than wheat flour.
6. Start the bread machine. Coconut flour bread dough will be thicker and less pourable than traditional wheat dough.
7. Once the baking cycle is complete, remove the bread and let it cool before slicing.

Per serving: Calories: 230kcal; Fat: 15g; Carbs: 22g; Protein: 8.5g

Nut-Free Sweet Potato Bread

Degree of difficulty: ★★☆☆☆ **Average expense:** $4-$5
Preparation time: 10 minutes **Servings:** 1.5 lb loaf (12 slices)

Ingredients:

- 1 1/4 cups warm water (at a temp. around 110 deg.F)
- 2 teaspoons active dry yeast
- 1 1/2 cups mashed sweet potatoes
- 1/2 cup sorghum flour
- 2 tablespoons olive oil
- 1/2 teaspoon salt

Directions:

1. Inside the bread machine pot, include warm water and olive oil.
2. Spray yeast across the water and allow it to relax for around 10 minutes until it becomes foamy.
3. Include mashed sweet potatoes, sorghum flour, and salt to the pan.
4. Select the gluten-free setting on your bread machine and start.
5. Allow the bread to cool prior to slicing.

Per serving: Calories: 120kcal; Fat: 3g; Carbs: 20g; Protein: 3g

FODMAP-Friendly Spelt Bread

Degree of difficulty: ★★☆☆☆ **Average expense:** $4-$5
Preparation time: 10 minutes **Servings:** 1.5 lb loaf (12 slices)

Ingredients:

- 1 1/4 cups warm water (at a temp. around 110 deg.F)
- 2 teaspoons active dry yeast
- 1 1/2 cups spelt flour
- 1/2 cup oat flour
- 2 tablespoons olive oil
- 1/2 teaspoon salt

Directions:

1. Inside the bread machine pot, include warm water and olive oil.
2. Spray yeast across the water and allow it to relax for around 10 minutes until it becomes foamy.
3. Include spelt flour, oat flour, and salt to the pan.
4. Select the basic/normal bread setting on your bread machine and start.
5. Allow the bread to cool prior to slicing.

Per serving: Calories: 110kcal; Fat: 3g; Carbs: 19g; Protein: 3g

Sibo Diet Cassava Bread

Degree of difficulty: ★★☆☆☆ **Average expense:** $5-$6

Preparation time: 10 minutes **Servings:** 1.5 lb loaf (12 slices)

Ingredients:

- 1 1/4 cups warm water (at a temp. around 110 deg.F)
- 2 teaspoons active dry yeast
- 1 1/2 cups cassava flour
- 1/2 cup coconut flour
- 2 tablespoons olive oil
- 1/2 teaspoon salt

Directions:

1. Inside the bread machine pot, include warm water and olive oil.
2. Spray yeast across the water and allow it to relax for around 10 minutes until it becomes foamy.
3. Include cassava flour, coconut flour, and salt to the pan.
4. Select the gluten-free setting on your bread machine and start.
5. Allow the bread to cool prior to slicing.

Per serving: Calories: 130kcal; Fat: 4.5g; Carbs: 20g; Protein: 2g

Mediterranean Diet Fig and Walnut Bread with Feta

Degree of difficulty: ★★★☆☆

Average expense: $5-$6

Preparation time: 20 minutes

Servings: 1.5 lb loaf (12 slices)

Ingredients:

- 1 1/4 cups warm water (at a temp. around 110 deg.F)
- 2 1/4 teaspoons active dry yeast
- 2 cups all-purpose flour
- 1 cup whole wheat flour
- 1/2 cup crumbled feta cheese
- 1/2 cup chopped dried figs
- 1/2 cup chopped walnuts
- 1/4 cup olive oil
- 1/2 teaspoon salt
- 1 tablespoon honey
- 1 teaspoon dried basil
- 1/2 teaspoon dried rosemary, crushed

Directions:

1. Add the warm water and honey to the bread machine pan. Sprinkle the yeast over the mixture and let it sit for about 5 minutes until frothy.
2. Add the all-purpose flour, whole wheat flour, olive oil, salt, basil, and rosemary to the pan.
3. Start the bread machine on the dough setting and let it mix the ingredients.
4. Once the dough has started to come together, add the crumbled feta cheese, chopped dried figs, and chopped walnuts.
5. After the dough cycle is complete, if the machine does not have a bake function, shape the dough into a loaf and place it in a greased bread pan. Allow it to rise in a warm place for about 30 minutes.
6. Preheat your oven to 350°F (175°C). Bake the bread for 30-40 minutes, or until it is golden brown.
7. Let the bread cool before slicing.

Per serving: Calories: 160kcal; Fat: 4g; Carbs: 2g; Protein: 7g

South Beach Diet Flaxseed Bread

Degree of difficulty: ★★☆☆☆ **Average expense:** $4-$5

Preparation time: 10 minutes **Servings:** 1.5 lb loaf (12 slices)

Ingredients:

- 1 1/4 cups warm water (at a temp. around 110 deg.F)
- 2 teaspoons active dry yeast
- 1 1/2 cups flaxseed meal
- 1/2 cup almond flour
- 2 tablespoons olive oil
- 1/2 teaspoon salt

Directions:

1. Inside the bread machine pot, include warm water and olive oil.
2. Spray yeast across the water and allow it to relax for around 10 minutes until it becomes foamy.
3. Include flaxseed meal, almond flour, and salt to the pan.
4. Select the gluten-free setting on your bread machine and start.
5. Allow the bread to cool prior to slicing.

Per serving: Calories: 120kcal; Fat: 9g; Carbs: 5g; Protein: 5g

Atkins Diet Cauliflower Bread

Degree of difficulty: ★★★☆☆ **Average expense:** $5-$5

Preparation time: 20 minutes **Servings:** 1.5 lb loaf (12 slices)

Ingredients:

- 1 1/4 cups warm water (at a temp. around 110 deg.F)
- 2 teaspoons active dry yeast
- 1 1/2 cups cauliflower rice (cooked and cooled)
- 1/2 cup almond flour
- 2 tablespoons olive oil
- 1/2 teaspoon salt

Directions:

1. Inside the bread machine pot, include warm water and olive oil.
2. Spray yeast across the water and allow it to relax for around 10 minutes until it becomes foamy.
3. Include cauliflower rice, almond flour, and salt to the pan.
4. Select the gluten-free setting on your bread machine and start.
5. Allow the bread to cool prior to slicing.

Per serving: Calories: 130kcal; Fat: 9g; Carbs: 7g; Protein: 5g

DASH Diet Multigrain Bread with Seeds and Nuts

Degree of difficulty: ★★☆☆☆ **Average expense:** $4-$5

Preparation time: 15 minutes **Servings:** 1.5 lb loaf (12 slices)

Ingredients:

- 1 1/4 cups warm water (at a temp. around 110 deg.F)
- 2 1/4 teaspoons active dry yeast
- 1 cup whole wheat flour
- 1/2 cup rolled oats
- 1/2 cup barley flour
- 1/4 cup flaxseed meal
- 1/4 cup chopped almonds
- 1/4 cup raw sunflower seeds
- 2 tablespoons honey
- 2 tablespoons olive oil
- 1/2 teaspoon salt (optional, can be reduced or omitted for lower sodium content)
- 1 teaspoon cinnamon (for a hint of sweetness without added sugar)

Directions:

1. Add the warm water to the bread machine pan. Sprinkle the yeast over the water and let it sit for about 5 minutes until frothy.
2. Add the whole wheat flour, rolled oats, barley flour, flaxseed meal, olive oil, honey, and salt (if using) to the pan.
3. Select the whole wheat bread setting on your bread machine.
4. As the machine begins to mix the ingredients, add the chopped almonds and sunflower seeds.
5. Let the machine complete the cycle.
6. Once the baking cycle is complete, remove the bread and let it cool before slicing.

Per serving: Calories: 130kcal; Fat: 7g; Carbs: 17g; Protein: 4g

Weight Watchers Friendly Chia and Honey Bread

Degree of difficulty: ★★☆☆☆ **Average expense:** $3-$4

Preparation time: 10 minutes **Servings:** 1.5 lb loaf (12 slices)

Ingredients:

- 1 1/4 cups warm water (at a temp. around 110 deg.F)
- 2 1/4 teaspoons active dry yeast
- 2 cups whole wheat flour
- 1/2 cup oat bran
- 1/4 cup chia seeds
- 1 tablespoon honey
- 2 tablespoons unsweetened applesauce
- 1/2 teaspoon salt

Directions:

1. Add the warm water to the bread machine pan. Sprinkle the yeast over the water and let it sit for about 5 minutes until frothy.
2. Add the whole wheat flour, oat bran, chia seeds, honey, unsweetened applesauce, and salt to the pa.
3. Select the 'whole wheat bread setting on your bread machine to accommodate the denser, whole grain ingredients.
4. Start the machine and let it run through the cycle.
5. Once the baking cycle is complete, remove the bread and let it cool before slicing.

Per serving: Calories: 110kcal; Fat: g; Carbs: 20g; Protein: 4g

High-Fiber Psyllium Bread

Degree of difficulty: ★★☆☆☆ **Average expense:** $2-$3
Preparation time: 10 minutes **Servings:** 1.5 lb loaf (12 slices)

Ingredients:

- 1 1/4 cups warm water (at a temp. around 110 deg.F)
- 2 teaspoons active dry yeast
- 1 1/2 cups whole wheat flour
- 1/2 cup psyllium husk
- 2 tablespoons olive oil
- 1/2 teaspoon salt

Directions:

1. Inside the bread machine pot, include warm water and olive oil.
2. Spray yeast across the water and allow it to relax for around 10 minutes until it becomes foamy.
3. Include whole wheat flour, psyllium husk, and salt to the pan.
4. Select whole wheat bread setting on your bread machine and start.
5. Allow the bread to cool prior to slicing.

Per serving: Calories: 120kcal; Fat: 3.5g; Carbs: 20g; Protein: 3g

Thyroid-Friendly Seaweed Bread

Degree of difficulty: ★★☆☆☆ **Average expense:** $4-$5
Preparation time: 10 minutes **Servings:** 1.5 lb loaf (12 slices)

Ingredients:

- 1 1/4 cups warm water (at a temp. around 110 deg.F)
- 2 teaspoons active dry yeast
- 1 1/2 cups spelt flour
- 1/2 cup dried seaweed flakes (such as nori)
- 2 tablespoons olive oil
- 1/2 teaspoon salt

Directions:

1. Inside the bread machine pot, include warm water and olive oil.
2. Spray yeast across the water and allow it to relax for around 10 minutes until it becomes foamy.
3. Include spelt flour, dried seaweed flakes, and salt to the pan.
4. Select the whole wheat setting on your bread machine and start.
5. Allow the bread to cool prior to slicing.

Per serving: Calories: 130kcal; Fat: 4g; Carbs: 20g; Protein: 4g

Celiac-Friendly Teff Bread

Degree of difficulty: ★★☆☆☆ **Average expense:** $4-$5

Preparation time: 10 minutes **Servings:** 1.5 lb loaf (12 slices)

Ingredients:

- 1 1/4 cups warm water (at a temp. around 110 deg.F)
- 2 teaspoons active dry yeast
- 1 1/2 cups teff flour
- 1/2 cup brown rice flour
- 2 tablespoons olive oil
- 1/2 teaspoon salt

Directions:

1. Inside the bread machine pot, include warm water and olive oil.
2. Spray yeast across the water and allow it to relax for around 10 minutes until it becomes foamy.
3. Include teff flour, brown rice flour, and salt to the pan.
4. Select the gluten-free setting on your bread machine and start.
5. Allow the bread to cool prior to slicing.

Per serving: Calories: 120kcal; Fat: 4g; Carbs: 20g; Protein: 3g

Anti-Inflammatory Turmeric Bread

Degree of difficulty: ★★☆☆☆ **Average expense:** $4-$5

Preparation time: 10 minutes **Servings:** 1.5 lb loaf (12 slices)

Ingredients:

- 1 1/4 cups warm water (at a temp. around 110 deg.F)
- 2 teaspoons active dry yeast
- 1 1/2 cups whole wheat flour
- 1/2 teaspoon ground turmeric
- 2 tablespoons olive oil
- 1/2 teaspoon salt
- 1/4 teaspoon black pepper (to enhance turmeric absorption)

Directions:

1. Inside the bread machine pot, include warm water and olive oil.
2. Spray yeast across the water and allow it to relax for around 10 minutes until it becomes foamy.
3. Include whole wheat flour, ground turmeric, salt, and black pepper to the pan.
4. Select the whole wheat bread setting on your bread machine and start.
5. Allow the bread to cool prior to slicing.

Per serving: Calories: 110kcal; Fat: 3.5g; Carbs: 19g; Protein: 3g

Dough Beyond Bread

This chapter is dedicated to the creative and sometimes surprising uses of your bread machine, extending its capabilities beyond the traditional loaves and into the world of culinary creativity.

Here, you'll discover recipes that transform simple dough into an array of delectable treats, ranging from sweet pastries to savory delights. We'll explore how your bread machine can become an indispensable ally in making perfect dough for pizzas, pretzel, cinnamon rolls, and even artisan pastries from around the globe.

Pizza Dough

Degree of difficulty: ★★☆☆☆ **Average expense:** $2-$8 (depending on the toppings)

Preparation time: 10 minutes **Servings:** 1 big pizza

Ingredients:

- 1 cup warm water (at a temp. around 110 deg.F)
- 2 1/4 teaspoons active dry yeast
- 2 1/2 cups whole wheat flour
- 1 teaspoon salt
- 2 tablespoons olive oil

Directions:

1. Put warm water in the bread machine pan.
2. Spray yeast across the water and allow it to relax for 5 minutes until it becomes frothy.
3. Bring whole wheat flour, salt, and olive oil to the pan.
4. Select dough setting on your bread machine and start it.
5. Once the cycle is complete, your pizza dough is ready to use. Roll it out, include your favorite toppings, then bake as desired.

Per serving: Calories: 300kcal; Fat: 5g; Carbs: 54g; Protein: 10g

Dinner Rolls

Degree of difficulty: ★★★☆☆ **Average expense:** $3-$4

Preparation time: 20 minutes **Servings:** 12 rolls

Ingredients:

- 1 cup warm milk (at a temp. around 110 deg.F)
- 2 tablespoons sugar
- 2 teaspoons active dry yeast
- 1/4 cup unsalted butter, melted
- 1 egg, beaten
- 3 1/4 cups all-purpose flour
- 1 teaspoon salt

Directions:

1. In the bread machine pan, combine the warm milk and sugar. Sprinkle the yeast over the mixture and let it sit for about 5 minutes until frothy.
2. Add the melted butter and beaten egg to the pan.
3. Add the all-purpose flour and salt.
4. Set the bread machine to the dough cycle and start it.
5. Once the cycle is complete, remove the dough from the pan and place it on a lightly floured surface.
6. Divide the dough into 12 equal portions and shape each into a ball.
7. Place the dough balls on a greased baking sheet, cover with a clean cloth, and let them rise in a warm place for about 30 minutes or until doubled in size.
8. Preheat your oven to 350°F (175°C).
9. Bake the rolls for 15-20 minutes or until golden brown.

Per serving: Calories: 180kcal; Fat: 5.5g; Carbs: 29g; Protein: 5g

Bagel Dough

Degree of difficulty: ★★★☆☆ **Average expense:** $2-$3
Preparation time: 20 minutes **Servings:** 6 bagels

Ingredients:

- 1 cup warm water (at a temp. around 110 deg.F)
- 2 1/4 teaspoons active dry yeast
- 3 cups bread flour
- 1 1/2 teaspoons salt
- 1 tablespoon honey
- 1 tablespoon olive oil

Directions:

1. Pour warm water into bread machine pan.
2. Spray yeast across the water and allow it to relax for 5 minutes.
3. Include bread flour, salt, honey, and olive oil to the pan.
4. Select dough setting on your bread machine and start it.
5. After the cycle is complete, divide the dough into 6 portions, shape them into bagels, and boil in water for 1-2 minutes.
6. Bake at 425 deg.F for 20-25 minutes until golden.

Per serving: Calories: 290kcal; Fat: 2g; Carbs: 58g; Protein: 8g

Spinach and Feta Stuffed Bread Dough

Degree of difficulty: ★★★☆☆

Average expense: $4-$5

Preparation time: 20 minutes

Servings: 1.5 lb loaf (12 slices)

Ingredients:

- 1 cup warm water (110 deg.F)
- 2 tablespoons olive oil
- 1 tablespoon sugar
- 1 teaspoon salt
- 3 cups all-purpose flour
- 1 1/2 teaspoons active dry yeast
- 1 teaspoon dried basil
- 1/2 teaspoon garlic powder
- 1 tablespoon olive oil
- 2 cups fresh spinach, chopped
- 1/2 cup feta cheese, crumbled
- 1/4 cup red onion, finely chopped
- 1/4 teaspoon black pepper
- 1/2 teaspoon dried oregano

Directions:

1. In the bread machine pan, add warm water, olive oil, and sugar.
2. Add flour, salt, dried basil, and garlic powder. Create a small indentation on top of the flour and add the yeast.
3. Select the dough cycle on your bread machine and start it.
4. While the dough is being prepared, heat 1 tablespoon of olive oil in a pan. Sauté the spinach and red onion until the spinach is wilted and the onion is soft. Let it cool.
5. Stir in the feta cheese, black pepper, and oregano into the spinach mixture.
6. Once the dough cycle is complete, roll out the dough on a floured surface into a large rectangle.
7. Spread the spinach and feta mixture evenly over the dough, leaving a small border around the edges.
8. Roll up the dough tightly, starting from the long edge, to enclose the filling.
9. Place the roll, seam side down, on a greased baking sheet. Make diagonal slits on the top of the roll.
10. Let it rise in a warm place for about 30 minutes.
11. Preheat your oven to 375°F (190°C).
12. Bake for 25-30 minutes, or until the bread is golden brown and sounds hollow when tapped.
13. Let it cool slightly before slicing.

Per serving: Calories: 200kcal; Fat: 6.5g; Carbs: 30g; Protein: 5g

Focaccia Dough

Degree of difficulty: ★★★☆☆ **Average expense:** $2-$3
Preparation time: 20 minutes **Servings:** 12-inch focaccia

Ingredients:

- 1 cup warm water (at a temp. around 110 deg.F)
- 2 1/4 teaspoons active dry yeast
- 2 1/2 cups all-purpose flour
- 1 teaspoon salt
- 2 tablespoons olive oil
- 1 teaspoon dried rosemary (elective)

Directions:

1. Put warm water in the bread machine pan.
2. Spray yeast across the water and allow it to relax for 5 minutes until frothy.
3. Bring all-purpose flour, salt, and olive oil to the pan.
4. Select dough setting on your bread machine and start it.
5. After the cycle, roll the dough into a 12-inch circle on a oiled baking sheet.
6. Press dimples into the dough, spray with olive oil, and spray with salt and rosemary.
7. Let it rise for 30 minutes, then bake at 400 deg.F for 20-25 minutes until golden.

Per serving: Calories: 200kcal; Fat: 3g; Carbs: 38g; Protein: 5g

English Muffin Dough

Degree of difficulty: ★★★☆☆ **Average expense:** $3-$4

Preparation time: 20 minutes **Servings:** 10 English muffins

Ingredients:

- 1 cup milk, warmed to 110 deg.F
- 2 tablespoons sugar
- 2 teaspoons active dry yeast
- 3 cups all-purpose flour
- 1 teaspoon salt
- 1/4 cup unsalted butter, melted
- 1 egg, beaten
- Cornmeal for dusting

Directions:

1. Add the warm milk to the bread machine pan. Sprinkle the sugar and yeast over the milk and let it sit for about 5 minutes until frothy.
2. Add the beaten egg and melted butter to the pan.
3. Add the all-purpose flour and salt.
4. Select the dough cycle on your bread machine and start it.
5. Once the cycle is complete, remove the dough and place it on a lightly floured surface.
6. Roll out the dough to about 1/2-inch thickness. Use a round cutter to cut out muffin shapes.
7. Sprinkle cornmeal on a baking sheet and place the cut dough pieces on it. Sprinkle the tops with more cornmeal.
8. Cover with a clean cloth and let them rise in a warm place for about 30 minutes.
9. Heat a skillet or griddle over medium heat. Cook the muffins for about 5-7 minutes on each side or until browned and cooked through.

Per serving: Calories: 210kcal; Fat: 6.5g; Carbs: 33g; Protein: 5g

Croissant Dough

Degree of difficulty: ★★★☆☆   **Average expense:** $2-$3
Preparation time: 20 minutes   **Servings:** 12 croissants

Ingredients:

- 1 cup warm milk
- 2 1/4 teaspoons active dry yeast
- 3 cups bread flour
- 1 tablespoon sugar
- 1 1/2 teaspoons salt
- 1/2 cup unsalted butter, softened

Directions:

1. Pour warm milk into the bread machine pan.
2. Spray yeast over the milk and let it proof for 5 minutes.
3. Include bread flour, sugar, and salt to the pan. Select dough setting and start.
4. Once the cycle is complete, roll out the dough, disperse softened butter, wrap, and chill for 30 minutes.
5. Roll out the dough again, cut into triangles, roll up, then bake at 375 deg.F for 15-20 minutes until golden.

Per serving: Calories: 230kcal; Fat: 11g; Carbs: 26g; Protein: 5g

Danish Pastry Dough

Degree of difficulty: ★★★☆☆   **Average expense:** $2-$3
Preparation time: 20 minutes   **Servings:** 12 pastries

Ingredients:

- 1 cup warm milk
- 2 1/4 teaspoons active dry yeast
- 2 1/2 cups all-purpose flour
- 1/4 cup sugar
- 1/2 teaspoon salt
- 1/2 cup unsalted butter, softened

Directions:

1. Pour warm milk into the bread machine pan.
2. Spray yeast over the milk and let it proof for 5 minutes.
3. Include all-purpose flour, sugar, salt, and softened butter to the pan. Select dough setting and start.
4. After the cycle is complete, roll out the dough, cut into squares, and fill with desired toppings. Wrap into triangles then bake at 375 deg.F for 15-20 minutes.

Per serving: Calories: 210kcal; Fat: 11g; Carbs: 24g; Protein: 4g

Whole Wheat Pita Bread with Flaxseed and Herbs Dough

Degree of difficulty: ★★★☆☆   **Average expense:** $4-$5

Preparation time: 20 minutes   **Servings:** 8 pitas

Ingredients:

- 1 cup warm water (110 deg.F)
- 2 tablespoons olive oil
- 2 cups whole wheat flour
- 1 cup all-purpose flour
- 2 tablespoons ground flaxseed
- 1 teaspoon dried oregano
- 1/2 teaspoon dried basil
- 1 teaspoon salt
- 2 1/4 teaspoons active dry yeast

Directions:

1. Place warm water and olive oil in the bread machine pan.
2. Add whole wheat flour, all-purpose flour, salt, dried Italian herbs, and minced garlic to the pan.
3. Make an indentation in the flour mixture and carefully add the yeast.
4. Select the dough cycle on your bread machine and start it.
5. Once the cycle is complete, divide the dough into 8 equal pieces. Roll each piece into a ball and then flatten with a rolling pin to form the pita shape.
6. Cover the flattened dough pieces with a clean cloth and let them rest for about 10 minutes.
7. Preheat your oven to 475°F (245°C) and place a baking stone or inverted baking sheet inside to heat.
8. Once the oven is heated, place the pitas on the hot baking stone or sheet. Bake for 3-5 minutes, or until they are puffed up and slightly golden.
9. Remove the pitas from the oven and cover them with a cloth to keep them soft.

Per serving: Calories: 200kcal; Fat: 4g; Carbs: 30g; Protein: g

Flatbread Dough

Degree of difficulty: ★★★☆☆ **Average expense:** $2-$3
Preparation time: 20 minutes **Servings:** 8-10 flatbreads

Ingredients:

- 1 cup warm water (at a temp. around 110 deg.F)
- 2 1/4 teaspoons active dry yeast
- 2 1/2 cups whole wheat flour
- 1/2 teaspoon salt
- 1 tablespoon olive oil

Directions:

1. Put warm water into the bread machine pan.
2. Spray yeast across the water and allow it to relax for 5 minutes.
3. Bring whole wheat flour, salt, and olive oil to the pan.
4. Select dough setting on your bread machine and start it.
5. Once the cycle is complete, divide the dough into 8-10 portions, roll them out, and cook in a dry griddle or griddle for 1-2 minutes on all sides.

Per serving: Calories: 120kcal; Fat: 2g; Carbs: 22g; Protein: 4g

Scone Dough

Degree of difficulty: ★★☆☆

Average expense: $3-$4

Preparation time: 20 minutes

Servings: 8 scones

Ingredients:

- 2 cups all-purpose flour
- 1/4 cup sugar
- 1 tablespoon baking powder
- 1/2 teaspoon salt
- 1/2 cup cold unsalted butter, cubed
- 1/2 cup cold milk
- 1 egg
- 1 teaspoon vanilla extract

Directions:

1. In the bread machine, include flour, sugar, baking powder, and salt.
2. Include the cubed cold butter to the machine.
3. Inside distinct container, mix cold milk, egg, and vanilla extract.
4. Put the wet components into the bread machine.
5. Select dough setting and start the machine.
6. Once the dough is ready, transfer it to a floured surface and shape into a circle. Cut into 8 wedges.
7. Bake scones at 400 deg.F for 12-15 minutes, until golden brown.

Per serving: Calories: 280kcal; Fat: 14g; Carbs: 34g; Protein: 5g

Thai Coconut Bread Dough

Degree of difficulty: ★★★☆☆ **Average expense:** $5-$6
Preparation time: 20 minutes **Servings:** 1.5 lb loaf (12 slices)

Ingredients:

- 1 cup coconut milk, warmed to 110 deg.F
- 1/4 cup water, warmed to 110 deg.F
- 2 1/4 teaspoons active dry yeast
- 3 cups all-purpose flour
- 1/2 cup shredded unsweetened coconut
- 1 tablespoon finely chopped lemongrass
- 1 teaspoon salt
- 2 tablespoons sugar
- 2 tablespoons melted coconut oil
- 1 egg, lightly beaten (for egg wash)

Directions:

1. In the bread machine pan, combine the warm coconut milk, water, and sugar. Sprinkle the yeast over the mixture and let it sit for about 5 minutes until frothy.
2. Add the all-purpose flour, shredded coconut, chopped lemongrass, salt, and melted coconut oil to the pan.
3. Set your bread machine to the dough cycle and start it.
4. Once the cycle is complete, remove the dough and place it on a lightly floured surface.
5. Shape the dough as desired – it can be formed into a loaf, rolls, or even twisted into artistic shapes.
6. Place the shaped dough on a baking sheet, cover with a clean cloth, and let it rise in a warm place for about 30-40 minutes.
7. Preheat your oven to 375°F (190°C).
8. Before baking, brush the dough lightly with the beaten egg for a glossy finish.
9. Bake for 20-25 minutes or until the bread is golden brown.

Per serving: Calories: 200kcal; Fat: 6g; Carbs: 30g; Protein: g

Dumpling Dough

Degree of difficulty: ★★★☆☆ **Average expense:** $1-$2

Preparation time: 10 minutes **Servings:** 20 dumplings

Ingredients:

- 2 cups all-purpose flour
- 1/2 teaspoon salt
- 1/2 cup water

Directions:

1. In the bread machine, include flour and salt.
2. Pour water into the machine.
3. Select dough setting and start the machine.
4. Once ready, roll it out on a floured surface then cut into circles using a round cutter or a glass.
5. Fill with your choice of dumpling filling (e.g., ground meat, vegetables, or sweet fillings).
6. Wrap dough over the filling, seal, and cook according to your preferred dumpling recipe.

Per serving: Calories: 40kcal; Fat: 0g; Carbs: 9g; Protein: 1g

Waffle Batter Dough

Degree of difficulty: ★★☆☆☆ **Average expense:** $3-$4

Preparation time: 15 minutes **Servings:** 6 waffles

Ingredients:

- 1 1/2 cups all-purpose flour
- 2 tablespoons sugar
- 1 tablespoon baking powder
- 1/4 teaspoon salt
- 2 big eggs
- 1 1/4 cups milk
- 1/4 cup vegetable oil

Directions:

1. In the bread machine, include flour, sugar, baking powder, and salt.
2. Bring eggs, milk, and vegetable oil to the machine.
3. Select dough setting and start the machine.
4. Once batter is ready, preheat your waffle iron then cook waffles according to the manufacturer's instructions.

Per serving: Calories: 260kcal; Fat: 10g; Carbs: 37g; Protein: 7g

Challenges, Mistakes, and Remedies

Bread baking, while incredibly rewarding, can be fraught with challenges, especially for beginners. In this chapter, we will explore the common mistakes made by novices and how to avoid them. We will also discuss how to tackle various bread failures, from dense loaves to uncooked centers, so you can troubleshoot and turn your baking mishaps into successful loaves.

Common Beginner Mistakes and How to Avoid Them

1. **Inaccurate Measurement**

Mistake: using imprecise measurements can lead to inconsistent results. Over or under-measuring flour, water, or yeast can affect the dough's texture and rise.

Remedy: invest in a kitchen scale for precise measurements. Follow your recipe carefully, using level measurements for dry components, and weigh wet components for accuracy.

2. **Using Incorrect Water Temperature**

Mistake: yeast is sensitive to temp. Water that is too hot could kill the yeast, while water that is too cold won't activate the yeast properly.

Remedy: use a kitchen thermometer to ensure your water is within the recommended temp. range, usually around 110 deg.F. The warm water should feel comfortable to the touch but not hot.

3. **Not Kneading Enough**

Mistake: inadequate kneading can result in a dense, crumbly loaf with an uneven texture.

Remedy: follow the kneading time recommended in your recipe or till the dough becomes smooth and elastic. Proper kneading ensures good gluten development.

4. **Rushing the Rising Time**

Mistake: patience is key when it comes to rising. Rushing the process can lead to underdeveloped flavor and a heavy texture.

Remedy: allow the dough to rise for the recommended duration. It should double in size during the first rise, and a shorter second rise is usually sufficient.

5. **Ignoring the Dough's Appearance**

Mistake: neglecting to monitor the dough's appearance during rising and kneading can result in under- or over-risen bread.

Remedy: keep an eye on your dough. It should double in size during rising, and when you press a finger into it, the indentation should slowly spring back.

6. **Not Greasing or Flouring Properly**

Mistake: failing to oil pans or properly flour work surfaces can cause the dough to stick, resulting in a deformed loaf.

Remedy: grease pans generously or use parchment paper to prevent sticking. Flour work surfaces adequately to facilitate shaping and handling the dough.

7. **Under baking**

Mistake: under baking the bread can lead to a gummy, uncooked center, and a lackluster crust.

Remedy: bake your bread till it sounds hollow when tapped on the bottom or reaches the appropriate internal temp., typically around 190 deg.F.

8. **Overbaking**

Mistake: baking the bread for too long can result in a dry and tough texture, as well as a burnt crust.

Remedy: follow the recommended baking times in your recipe and monitor the bread in the oven or on the pan to prevent overbaking. Cover the bread with foil if the crust is browning too quickly.

9. **Skipping the Resting Period**

Mistake: neglecting the resting period after baking can cause the bread to release excessive steam, making the crust less crispy.

Remedy: allow your bread to rest for almost 10-15 minutes after removing it from the oven. This lets the moisture redistribute, resulting in a better texture.

Tackling Bread Failures: From Dense Loaves to Uncooked Centers

1. **Dense Loaf**

Cause: dense loaves are often the result of under-kneading, over-flouring, or insufficient rising.

Remedy: for under-kneaded dough, knead longer till the dough is smooth and elastic. Reduce the flour if you suspect it's too much. Ensure you allow the dough to rise properly, doubling in size.

2. **Uncooked Center**

Cause: an uncooked center typically results from under baking or an overly big loaf.

Remedy: bake the bread for a longer duration, checking for doneness by tapping it and ensuring the internal temp. reaches around 190 deg.F. For oversized loaves, consider dividing the dough and baking it separately.

3. **Flat, Sunken Loaf**

Cause: a flat or sunken loaf can be attributed to over-rising, using too much yeast, or under-kneading.

Remedy: reduce the rising time, use less yeast, and ensure you knead the dough adequately. Over-rising can cause the dough to lose its structure and collapse.

4. **Burnt Crust**

Cause: a burnt crust often results from excessive baking time or too high of an oven temp.

Remedy: reduce the baking time and temp., covering the bread with foil if needed. Monitor the bread closely to avoid further burning.

5. **Crumbly Texture**

Cause: a crumbly texture can be due to over-baking or using too much flour.

Remedy: reduce the baking time and the amount of flour in your recipe. A crumbly texture can also be caused by using too much fat or sugar; adjust these components as needed.

6. **Sourdough Troubles**

Cause: sourdough bread can present unique challenges, including issues with the starter's activity or temp. fluctuations during fermentation.

Remedy: maintain a healthy sourdough starter with regular feedings and proper temp. control. Experiment with different fermentation times and temp. to achieve the desired flavor and texture.

7. **Sticky Dough**

Cause: sticky dough can result from using too much liquid or not allowing the dough to rest prior to shaping.

Remedy: reduce the liquid if the dough is too sticky. Rest the dough for around 10-15 minutes prior to shaping to allow the flour to fully hydrate and make handling easier.

Connecting with the Bread-Making Community

Bread baking is not just a solitary pursuit; it is a communal endeavor where enthusiasts, beginners, and seasoned bakers come together to share their experiences, knowledge, and passion for the craft. In this chapter, we'll explore the ways you can connect with the bread-making community, from websites and blogs to forums and podcasts, as well as influencers who can inspire and guide you on your baking journey.

Websites, Blogs, and Forums: Your Go-To Online Resources

The internet is a treasure trove of information and a place where the bread-making community thrives. Whether you are seeking recipes, troubleshooting advice, or simply looking for inspiration, these online resources have got you covered:

1. **The Fresh Loaf (thefreshloaf.com):** this community-driven website is a hub for bread bakers of all levels. It features forums for discussions, an extensive collection of recipes, and a valuable "Handbook" section filled with bread-baking tips and techniques.
2. **King Arthur Baking Company (kingarthurbaking.com):** King Arthur Flour is renowned for its quality products, and their website offers an array of tested recipes, guides, and baking tips. They also have a bustling online community with forums for sharing experiences and seeking advice.
3. **Breadtopia (breadtopia.com):** Breadtopia is a haven for those interested in artisan and sourdough bread. The website boasts a variety of tutorials, recipes, and videos, making it a valuable resource for both beginners and experienced bakers.
4. **The Perfect Loaf (theperfectloaf.com):** Maurizio Leo, the creator of The Perfect Loaf, shares his passion for sourdough bread baking through detailed guides and tutorials. His site is a fantastic resource for those who want to delve deep into the world of sourdough.
5. **Reddit Breadit (reddit.com/r/Breadit):** Reddit's Breadit is a vibrant community where bread enthusiasts gather to share their creations, ask questions, and engage in discussions. It's a fantastic platform for getting quick answers and inspiration.
6. **Facebook "Delicious Bread Machine Recipes":** this group has more than 100k subscribers that shares recipes, advices and common troubles. If you are a fan of bread making machine, you have to visit this group.

Podcasts and Influencers to Inspire Your Baking Journey

Podcasts are a great way to learn more about bread baking while multitasking or simply relaxing. These podcasts offer a wealth of knowledge and inspiration:

1. **"The Rye Baker Podcast (theryebaker.com)":** Stan Ginsberg, author of "The Rye Baker" and a passionate rye bread baker, explores the unique world of rye-based bread in this podcast. If you are interested in delving into the depths of rye, this is a must-listen.
2. **"The King Arthur Baking Show (kingarthurbaking.com/learn):** King Arthur Flour's podcast offers valuable insights and tips for both beginner and experienced bakers. It is an extension of their mission to share the joy of baking.

In addition to podcasts, there are influencers across various platforms who can guide and inspire you on your bread-making journey:

Instagram

- **@maurizio (Maurizio Leo):** Maurizio Leo shares his stunning sourdough creations, insights, and tutorials on Instagram.

YouTube

- **Bake with Jack:** Jack Sturgess, a professional baker, offers a plethora of bread-making tutorials, from basic recipes to more advanced techniques.

Pinterest

- Pinterest is a fantastic platform to discover bread recipes, techniques, and visual inspiration. Create boards and explore the endless possibilities of bread.

TikTok

- TikTok features a growing community of bakers who share short and snappy videos with tips, tricks, and recipes. Search for #breadmaking or #sourdough to uncover a treasure trove of content.

Conclusion: Embracing the Bread-Making Journey

As we conclude our exploration of the art and science of bread making, it is important to reflect on the profound journey you have embarked upon. Bread baking is more than a culinary pursuit; it is a delightful blend of tradition, creativity, and science. In the preceding chapters, we have covered the joys of homemade bread, the ins and outs of bread machines, the significance of components, the organic and budget-friendly approach, bread baking basics, common mistakes and remedies, and the vast network of the bread-making community. This knowledge equips you to create loaves that not only nourish the body but also warm the soul.

The Art and Science of Bread: A Beautiful Balance

Bread making is a unique convergence of art and science. The artistry lies in the baker's hands, shaping, scoring, and creating a signature touch that makes each loaf distinct. The science lies in the precision of measurements, the alchemy of yeast and fermentation, and the intricacies of gluten development. Balancing these elements is what turns a basic recipe into a culinary masterpiece. The aromas that fill your kitchen as the dough rises, the anticipation of the first slice, and the satisfaction of sharing a warm, freshly baked loaf with loved ones are the artful rewards of your effort.

In each loaf you create, there is a story waiting to be told. The story of a simple, yet profound transformation. From humble components to a perfectly risen, aromatic, and golden-brown creation, every step is a testament to your passion, patience, and skill. It is the story of a process that has been carried out for millennia, connecting you with bakers across time and cultures. And it is the story of the flavors, textures, and experiences you create for yourself and those you share your bread with.

Encouraging Continuous Learning and Experimentation

Your journey in bread making is far from over; in fact, it's just beginning. Embracing the world of bread baking is an ongoing adventure, a delightful pursuit that will continue to surprise, challenge, and inspire you. As you move forward, keep these guiding principles in mind:

1. **Never Stop Learning:** the world of bread is vast, and there is always something new to discover. Whether it is experimenting with different flours, exploring unique components, or mastering advanced techniques, your learning journey will never end.
2. **Embrace Mistakes:** every baker, no matter their level of expertise, makes mistakes. These are not failures but valuable lessons. Once a loaf does not turn out as expected, view it as an opportunity to grow and improve.
3. **Experiment and Innovate:** don't be afraid to break away from the tried-and-true recipes. Experiment with flavors, shapes, and techniques. Innovation is what keeps bread baking exciting and dynamic.
4. **Share Your Knowledge:** as you learn and grow, share your knowledge with others. Offer guidance to beginners, engage in discussions in online forums, and inspire new bakers to join the community. Your experience can be a beacon for someone else's journey.
5. **Stay Connected:** the bread-making community is a vast and welcoming one. Engage with bakers from around the world through websites, forums, and social media platforms. You will find camaraderie, encouragement, and inspiration.
6. **Celebrate the Journey:** the joy of bread baking is not solely in the final product but in the entire process. Savor the moments of kneading, the anticipation of rising, and the warmth of a just-baked loaf. Your journey is a source of fulfillment in itself.

In conclusion, bread making is an art that invites you to create, share, and connect. It is a science that beckons you to understand and master the intricate processes that turn flour and water into sustenance and delight. It's a journey that celebrates the journey itself, the learning, the experimenting, and the community. So, embrace the bread-making journey with open arms, a curious mind, and a willing heart. And remember, with each loaf you bake, you are not only nourishing the body but also feeding the soul. Happy baking!

Appendix

Glossary of Bread-Making Terms

Amish Friendship Bread starter: is similar to a normal sourdough starter but with the adding of sugar and milk.

Aroma: the pleasant and distinctive scent or fragrance produced by freshly baked bread, which plays a vital role in evoking emotions and memories.

Bread Machine: a kitchen appliance designed to automate the bread-making process, including mixing, kneading, rising, and baking, providing convenience and consistent results.

Bread Pan: the container inside a bread machine where the components are placed for the baking process.

Crust Color: a setting on a bread machine that allows the user to choose the desired color of the bread's crust, typically light, medium, or dark.

Digital Scale: a kitchen tool used for precise measurement of components by weight, ensuring accuracy in baking.

Dough: a solution of flour, water, yeast, and other components that is kneaded and allowed to rise prior to baking, forming the basis of bread.

Fermentation: the process by which yeast consumes sugars and produces carbon dioxide, leading to the rising of the bread.

Gluten Formation: the development of a protein network in the dough when gluten proteins in the flour interact with water, providing structure and elasticity to the bread.

Meniscus: the curved surface of a liquid inside a measuring container, which should be observed at eye level when measuring liquids for accuracy.

Monoculture: the practice of growing a single crop over an extensive area, which can have negative environmental impacts.

Sourdough Starter: a natural yeast culture used in sourdough bread making.

Wild Yeast: yeast naturally occurring in the environment, captured and cultivated for bread making, contributing to unique flavors and textures in sourdough bread.

Unbleached Flour: flour that has not undergone a bleaching process, often considered a better choice for bread making due to its superior qualities.

Yeast: a microorganism responsible for fermentation in bread making, leading to the rising of the dough and the development of bread's flavor and texture.

Conversion Table

Volume Equivalents (Liquid)

US Standard	US Standard (oz.)	Metric (approximate)
2 tablespoons	1 fl. oz.	30 milliliter
¼ cup	2 fl. oz.	60 milliliter
½ cup	4 fl. oz.	120 milliliter
1 cup	8 fl. oz.	240 milliliter
1½ cups	12 fl. oz.	360 milliliter
2 cups or 1 pint	16 fl. oz.	480 milliliter
4 cups or 1 quart	32 fl. oz.	960 milliliter

Volume Equivalents (Dry)

US Standard	Metric (approximate)
⅛ teaspoon	0.6 milliliter
¼ teaspoon	1.2 milliliter
½ teaspoon	2.5 milliliter
¾ teaspoon	3.7 milliliter
1 teaspoon	5 milliliter
1 tablespoon	15 milliliter
¼ cup	60 milliliter
⅓ cup	80 milliliter
½ cup	120 milliliter
⅔ cup	160 milliliter
¾ cup	180 milliliter
1 cup	240 milliliter
2 cups or 1 pint	480 milliliter
3 cups	720 milliliter
4 cups or 1 quart	960 milliliter

Oven Temperatures

Fahrenheit (F)	Celsius (C) (approximate)
110 deg.F	43 deg.C
250 deg.F	121 deg.C
300 deg.F	149 deg.C
325 deg.F	163 deg.C
350 deg.F	175 deg.C
375 deg.F	190 deg.C
400 deg.F	200 deg.C
425 deg.F	220 deg.C
450 deg.F	230 deg.C

Weight Equivalents

US Standard	Metric (approximate)
1 tablespoon	15 g
½ oz.	15 g
1 oz.	30 g
2 oz.	60 g
4 oz.	120 g
8 oz.	225 g
12 oz.	340 g
16 oz. or 1 lb.	455 g

Printed in Great Britain
by Amazon